FROM CASABLANCA TO BERLIN

Here is a vivid account of Allied fighting in the European and Mediterranean Theaters of World War II. Mr. Bliven traces the course of the conflict from the first American landings in North Africa to the unconditional surrender of Nazi Germany.

RANDOM HOUSE · NEW YORK

Landmark
BOOKS

Illustrated
with photographs

FROM CASABLANCA TO BERLIN

The War in North Africa and Europe: 1942-1945

by BRUCE BLIVEN, Jr.

For FREDERIC BRUCE BLIVEN

CONTENTS

PHOTOGRAPHIC SECTIONS

MAPS

THE WAR IN NORTH AFRICA

U.S. soldiers in a landing barge headed for Algeria. *(Wide World)*

American troops transfer from transports to assault boats for the North African landings. *(U.S. Army)*

Americans wade ashore at a North African beach. *(U.S. Army)*

Three Yanks dig in at an outpost near Oran. *(U.S. Army)*

General Bernard Law Montgomery, commander of the British Eighth Army. *(Imperial War Museum)*

German General Erwin Rommel (right), "the Desert Fox." *(U.S. Army)*

Some Rangers work out a tactical problem behind the lines in North Africa. *(U.S. Army)*

Remains of a tent hit during a German bombing raid on an Allied airfield in North Africa. *(U.S. Army)*

An M-3 tank of the 1st Armored Division advances to strengthen Allied positions at the Kasserine Pass, Tunisia. *(U.S. Army)*

General Eisenhower jokes with four GIs during an inspection tour of the Tunisian battlefront. *(Wide World)*

1
NORTH AFRICAN LANDINGS

Well before dawn the landing craft, loaded with American soldiers, stopped circling in the water and headed full speed for the beaches. The place: the coast of French Morocco on the sloping, northwestern shoulder of North Africa. The date: November 8, 1942.

The Second World War was more than three years old. The United States, however, had been in it for only eleven months—since December 7, 1941, when Japan's surprise attack on the U.S. naval base at Pearl Harbor, Hawaii, had put a sudden end to the country's efforts to stay neutral. Japan's European partners, Germany and Italy, had declared war against the United States four days later. The vast conflict between these three nations and Great Britain, the United States, the Soviet Union, and China encircled the globe.

Great Britain and the United States were concentrating first on helping Russia defeat Germany and Italy. After victory in Europe they planned to turn their full attention to the defeat of Japan. But up to now, the Americans' land battles had all been in the Pacific: a losing fight to keep the Japanese from capturing the Philippines and a successful fight in conjunction with the Australians to hold on to the east end of New Guinea. The U.S. Marines had also established a small beachhead on Guadalcanal Island, in the Solomons. Wheather or not they could defend it remained to be seen.

The North African landings—if they succeeded— would mark a great moment in United States military history. But first-wave assault troops don't think much about making history. They have too many other things on their minds. These infantrymen, dressed in herringbone-twill fatigue uniforms and wearing U.S. flag armbands, were intent on the shore ahead. They crouched low in the LCVPs (Landing Craft, Vehicle and Personnel) to avoid the spray and, if there were to be any, bullets. About thirty men rode in each boat, including an officer or two. They were weighted down with equipment—rifles, ammunition, hand grenades, entrenching tools, and canteens filled with water. They carried heavy packs on their backs—some weighing as many as sixty pounds. The ocean, which had looked calm enough from the transports' decks the night before, now seemed rough. The assault boats pitched and yawed with the Atlantic's never-ceasing swells. The soldiers knew that they might have trouble with the breaking surf when they came to the beaches.

The invisible coast was quiet. If the defending forces expected the landing, they hadn't reacted. Blinking lights on United States scout boats that had gone ahead to mark the LCVPs' courses were about all the men could see ahead. The run in to the beaches was expected to take about twenty minutes. If, despite the silence from the shore, the enemy was waiting, the Americans would find out very soon.

The soldiers were keyed up, like runners before a race. They had never been in combat before and they were as much afraid of the unknown experience as they were of being killed or wounded. Would combat prove so terrible they could not bear it? No one knew exactly how he would react, and waiting to find out had been a strain. The troops had been through months of training, maneuvers, and practice landings. Then they had sailed, combat-loaded and ready to go, all the way from Norfolk, Virginia, across the Atlantic. Cooped up in their crowded transport ships, they had yearned to feel solid earth under their feet again. Action—even dangerous action—promised some relief.

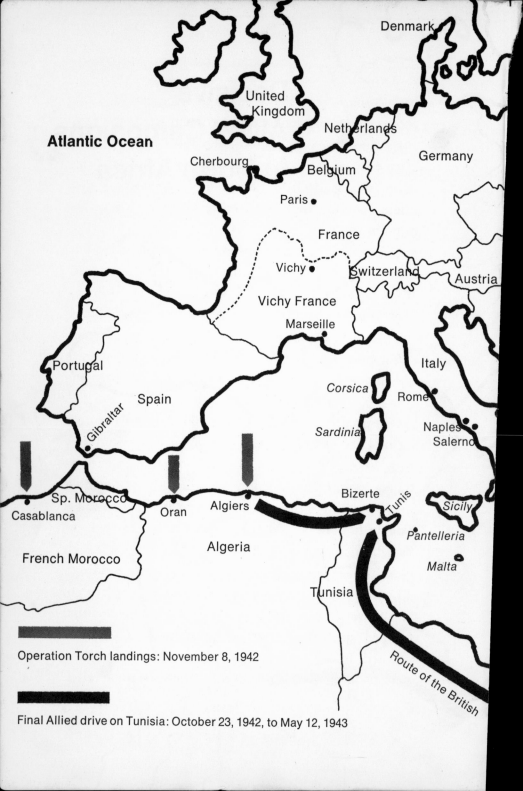

Operation Torch landings: November 8, 1942

Final Allied drive on Tunisia: October 23, 1942, to May 12, 1943

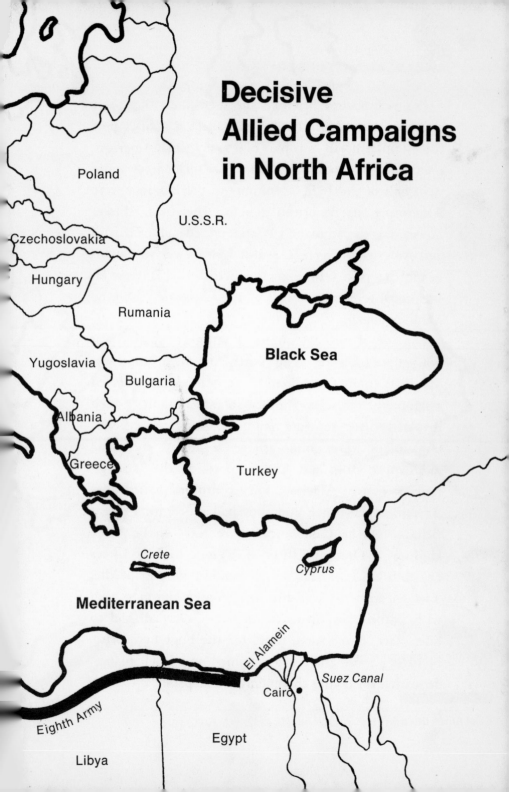

Decisive Allied Campaigns in North Africa

Poland

U.S.S.R.

Czechoslovakia

Hungary

Rumania

Black Sea

Yugoslavia

Bulgaria

Albania

Greece

Turkey

Crete

Cyprus

Mediterranean Sea

El Alamein

Suez Canal

Cairo

Eighth Army

Egypt

Libya

From shipboard briefings the men knew that their attack on Casablanca by way of Fedala, a smaller port fifteen miles north, was part of a vast British-American operation. Its code name was TORCH. Since more than half of the 107,000 soldiers in the landings were Americans, an American general, Dwight D. Eisenhower, was in command. With a mixed staff of British and American officers, General Eisenhower was at his headquarters at Gibraltar, the British rock-fortress on the narrow strait between the Atlantic and the Mediterranean.

Outside of military circles, Eisenhower's name was not yet well known. The North African invasion was his first combat command. It was a complicated assignment. Besides the Casablanca assault, which involved three separate landings, other amphibious task forces were going ashore at almost the same moment at Oran and Algiers, ports on the Mediterranean coast of Algeria. They combined British and American personnel, and they had sailed from Great Britain. As at Casablanca, there were to be three landings at Oran and three at Algiers: flanking forces on both sides of the troops landing in the middle. That meant a total of nine coördinated landings, each with peculiar problems of its own. They all had to take place at the same time, for the huge enterprise, involving more than 400 warships and 1,000 planes, depended on taking the enemy by surprise.

As the first-wave boats sped toward shore, brilliant searchlights at both ends of the beach suddenly split the dark sky. Their beams were first pointed upward; the roar of the incoming LCVPs had been mistaken for airplane engines. Almost immediately the lights were lowered and pointed out to sea, picking out the invasion fleet, ship by ship. Near the searchlights were powerful coast-defense guns—six, of them on Cape Fedala on the right, and four on Cherqui Point, the headland on the left. These guns were capable of wrecking the entire invasion plan.

The searchlights, which acted as the coast-artillery gunners' eyes, had to be put out. As soon as the lights found the ships, the destroyers *Wilkes*, *Swanson*, *Ludlow* and *Murphy* fired on them. The lights went out as suddenly as they had been turned on. Minutes later, in the welcome darkness, the leading assault boats touched land. The time was about 5:30 A.M. The first infantrymen, mostly members of the 3rd Infantry Division, began to scramble ashore.

The attack was obviously no longer a surprise. Still, an all-important question remained to be answered: would the French, who were manning the defenses at all nine of the assault points, fight back? Morocco and Algeria were still being run by Frenchmen, not Germans. This was in accord with the armistice France had signed after her defeat by Germany in the late spring of 1940. There were German armistice commissioners in Morocco and Algeria, checking up on French soldiers, sailors, and airmen, and on French government officials. These German commissioners wanted to make sure the French administrators were obeying the orders they received from the French puppet government at Vichy, France. The German and Italian armed forces in North Africa, however, were fully occupied in the desert far to the east, fighting the British.

Now the British-American landings were testing French loyalties as they had not been tested before. Would the French soldiers and sailors obey German orders, and shoot at their friends and former allies? The British and Americans hoped not, but feared the worst. The Allies had not been able to warn the French, except through secret diplomatic negotiations, lest they tell the Germans about the plan to attack. If the French decided to defend their coastline with all their might, their Moroccan and Algerian army, 100,000 men strong, could prove hard to beat. And the French navy in African waters, though small, was powerful. The French battleship *Jean Bart*, for example, was capable of firing all the way from Casablanca's harbor, where she lay, to Fedala Bay. One of her fifteen-inch shells could pulverize an assault boat.

At 6:00 A.M. the question was answered, and the answer was not the one the Allies had hoped for. The guns at Cape Fedala and Cherqui Point began to fire.

The French were going to resist.

United States destroyers fired back. The cruiser *Brooklyn,* racing in from her patrolling position offshore, sent up an observer in her tiny spotting plane to direct the fire of her six-inch guns. The *Brooklyn* began shooting at 6:22. Within minutes she hit the Cherqui battery's electronic fire-control equipment. The French guns could no longer be operated as a unit, by remote control, but had to be fired individually, by hand, which was slower and less effective. Not long after, the *Brooklyn* hit one of the concrete emplacements, putting the gun inside it out of action.

Meanwhile, during the hour from 5:00 to 6:00 A.M., the worst fears of the first-wave troops had been coming true. Many of the assault boats had difficulty finding their way to their assigned beaches. Some boats were thousands of yards off target, swept out of control by the heavy surf. Instead of making smooth landings on sand, they were hitting rocks and submerged reefs. Scores of the boats were smashed. Others capsized. The men in them were thrown into deep water. It was almost impossible to swim in shoes and ammunition belts. A few got rid of their heavy loads in time to save their lives. Hundreds drowned. Out of its thirty-one assault boats, one battalion lost twenty-two craft.

Some 3rd Division units, supposed to land more or less together, were scattered over a distance of a mile

9

or more. Men with weapons landed without ammunition. Radios were lost, or wouldn't work. Nonetheless, by the time the sun came up, thousands of American infantrymen were safely ashore. A number of companies were in reasonably good shape and, despite the mishaps, were hurrying on with their missions.

On the right side of the beach, the 1st Battalion of the 7th Infantry Regiment organized itself quickly. Colonel Roy E. Moore was its commander. The battalion's job was to capture the town of Fedala on the neck of the cape. It covered the 2,000 yards to the built-up area so quickly that the one defending outfit in the place, a company of Senegalese soldiers, was taken prisoner before it got set to fight. Ten German members of the Armistice Commission staying at the Hotel Miramar rushed out of the building just before the Americans entered it. They didn't get far. Nine of them were caught before their cars reached the highway to Rabat. By 6:00 A.M., Moore's men controlled Fedala.

On the left end of the beach most of the members of four infantry companies, with one mortar section, had been put ashore thousands of yards to the left of where they should have landed. They were on the wrong side of Cherqui Point. It might have taken them half the morning to move sideways to their proper starting place. Instead, using their own initiative, they attacked the damaged Cherqui Point guns.

The landing error was turned into an asset. When the *Brooklyn* stopped shelling, they lobbed 81-millimeter mortar shells ahead of themselves as they advanced against the other guns' concrete emplacements. This improvised thrust from the back side of the point coincided with the planned attack from the opposite direction. The French gun crews, finding infantrymen approaching from both sides, surrendered at 7:30.

The Cape Fedala guns were still firing. The cruiser *Augusta*, with the American ground forces commander, General George S. Patton, Jr., aboard, went into action. The flagship bombarded the Fedala batteries with its eight-inch shells for fifteen minutes. The Cape guns were silenced temporarily, but that wasn't enough. They had to be captured or destroyed. The navy gunners were forced to be cautious, because a high shot might clear the Cape and land in the town. The gunners didn't want to hurt any of Colonel Moore's men. In addition, there were oil-storage tanks near the guns. The Americans wanted to avoid hitting the tanks, for they hoped to use them later. It looked as if infantry would have to do the job.

A heavy antiaircraft battery, which could be fired against men on the ground, blocked the way. Colonel Moore's leading platoons, trying to approach the Cape guns from the rear, were pinned down. Before they could move ahead, the antiaircraft battery would have to be eliminated. A well-aimed missile from an anti-tank bazooka accomplished part of the job, but it was nearly 11:00 A.M. before the antiaircraft battery was knocked out. Then there was a forty-minute wait for a second naval bombardment of the tip of Cape Fedala, where expert shooting by the Cape guns was making the landing of men and supplies difficult.

As noon approached, an attack got moving: four light tanks supported Company A of the 7th Regiment. Colonel William H. Wilbur, one of General Patton's staff officers, inspired the advance. Wilbur had already put in a long day's work, but his first efforts had not been successful. One of the first ashore, Wilbur had driven at top speed through the enemy lines into Casablanca in a jeep draped with a huge white flag of truce. He had been hoping to persuade the French, particularly Vice Admiral François Michelier, who was commanding the Moroccan Naval Forces, not to resist. Unfortunately, by the time Wilbur reached the handsome Admiralty building, Michelier had already made up his mind to fight. In fact, the Casablanca guns, including the batteries of the *Jean Bart,* had just opened fire. They were being answered by the *Massachusetts,* the *Wichita,* and the *Tuscaloosa,* and the smoke of battle had begun to obscure Casablanca in a great cloud.

On his way back to report to Patton, Wilbur saw that the Cape Fedala guns were still firing. He also found that the *Augusta* hadn't yet put the General ashore. So Wilbur decided to try to help Company A's advance. He climbed on top of one of the tanks, making himself a ridiculously conspicuous target. From that daredevil vantage point, Wilbur directed the maneuver. Before long, Company A had fought its way into the gun emplacements, seized the Cape Fedala fire-control station, and captured the main battery of big guns. Twenty-two French prisoners were taken. By 3:00 P.M. the Cape Fedala guns were all quiet. For his day's work Colonel Wilbur won the highest United States military decoration, the Congressional Medal of Honor.

Charged with the protection of the assaulting troops, the U.S. Navy was meanwhile fighting a stiff battle. Twenty minutes after the cruisers started dueling with the *Jean Bart,* the French battleship was hit on her main battery. The damage kept her out of action for the next two days. But seven French destroyers, making a heavy smoke screen for themselves, had fought their way out of Casablanca harbor. They hoped to smash through the screen of warships to attack Allied transports and landing craft. Before long a light cruiser, the *Primauguet,* and eight French submarines joined them.

The Allied combination of naval and air strength was too much for the French. The *Augusta,* the *Brooklyn,* and two destroyers held them off: the American gunfire was faster, heavier, and more accurate than the French. One U.S. destroyer, the *Ludlow*, and several landing craft were hit, but four of the French destroyers and the *Primauguet* were sunk. By the end of the afternoon, the Fedala beachhead was secure.

General Patton was ashore. By his own schedule, he had landed six hours late. Worse, only a tiny fraction—less than two per cent—of the all-important supplies had been unloaded. This meant that the second phase of the attack, the move on Casablanca itself, would be delayed. There was a brief, false glimmer of hope: the French commandant of Fedala felt positive that the French resistance had been a mistake. Patton sent Major General Hobart S. Gay, under a flag of truce, to talk to Admiral Michelier. Gay fared worse than Wilbur. Michelier wouldn't even see him. Patton had to proceed with the original plan: to take Casablanca by force.

The news Patton received from Safi, the landing place 150 miles south of Casablanca, sounded good. Safi was important to the whole attack because it was the only port with large enough facilities to berth the United States tank carrier *Lakehurst*. The Americans could land medium tanks there and nowhere else on the Moroccan coast, and that was what they were doing. Combat Command B, a part of General Ernest Harmon's 2nd Armored Division, was being put ashore quickly. The plan called for the 2nd Armored to push north to Casablanca to attack the city from the south side. It had a long way to go, but it was off to a good start.

The news from the coast at Mehdia, the northern-most of the three landings, was not so good. Mehdia was proving unexpectedly tough. It had to be captured because it commanded the Port Lyautey airport inside a great U-shaped bend in the Sebou River nine miles upstream. P-40s brought in by the carriers *Chenango* and *Sangamon,* and other planes flown in from Gibraltar, should have been using the airstrip by late on D-Day. But, as darkness fell, Mehdia wasn't even under firm control, let alone the airfield.

Meanwhile the two landings on the Mediterranean coast were making progress. Although landing schedules at Oran and Algiers had also been badly scrambled, solid beachheads had been established. Neither port was yet in Allied hands, but Eisenhower had reason to hope that within two or three days they would be.

The following day, November 9th, was spent unscrambling the snarls of the 8th. The 3rd Division moved south from Fedala, getting into position for the final attack on Casablanca. French resistance was amazingly light. But the failure the day before to get supporting weapons, jeeps, trucks, and communications equipment ashore soon brought the leading infantry battalions to a halt. General Harmon's 2nd Armored column, moving up from Safi, ran into one

15

problem after another. The French were attempting to reinforce the Safi garrison and they had to be beaten back, or at least blocked off, before the 2nd Armored's drive toward Casablanca could proceed.

At Mehdia the question was whether the Allies could hang on to the precarious toe hold they had won the day before. The French were concentrating their defensive strength there. They threw a light-tank counterattack—two battalions of French infantry and eighteen Renault tanks—against the Americans' southern flank.

General Lucian K. Truscott, Jr., commanding the American operation, had only seven light tanks ashore. Their radios were out of order, and the sights on their 37-millimeter guns needed readjustment. Nevertheless, they took advantage of a slight rise in the ground near the main highway, and stopped the advancing French column. Though their shooting was inaccurate, the tanks' armor plate was too tough for the French guns. The French attack was stopped. Then naval fire from the light cruiser *Savannah* started falling on the French with demoralizing accuracy. They withdrew.

Another day went by. Then, on November 10th, the U.S. destroyer-transport *Dallas* attempted a daring feat of seamanship. Her 22-year-old commander, Robert J. Brodie, was going to try to take his ship from Mehdia up the shallow, treacherous Sebou River, all the way around the great horseshoe bend. If successful, he would land a 75-man infantry raiding party at the airport. The leading platoons of the 9th Infantry Division, which were advancing overland, needed help.

One mile from the mouth of the Sebou there was a heavy wire barrier-boom. Brodie thought it had been cut and opened in the middle of the night by a demolitions party. But when the *Dallas* approached the barrier at 5:30 A.M., Brodie realized that it was only partly open. The *Dallas* would have to try to ram her way through.

No one needed to tell Brodie or his crew what the cost of failure would be. If the *Dallas* got stuck on the barrier, ran aground on a sandbank, or hit any of the sunken wreckage in the river channel, she would be a sitting-duck target for the French artillery. There was plenty of it. Besides the coastal guns, especially the five-inch battery at the Kasba fortress guarding the mouth of the Sebou, the French had several other big guns capable of hitting the *Dallas* almost anywhere along her nine-mile route.

It wasn't safe to stop even long enough to think about the closed barrier. Brodie ordered the *Dallas* to proceed. The wheel of the ship was in the hands of a Moroccan river pilot, spirited out of the country some time earlier by the Office of Strategic Services (O.S.S.), America's secret intelligence and operations agency. The sharp bow of the *Dallas* smashed into the barrier and cut through it. Shells from the Kasba fortress were falling all around the ship. The river was just barely deep enough for the *Dallas;* the muddy bottom sucked at her hull. Brodie kept going. Heavy machine-gun fire from the river banks and the hills near the airport raked the ship's deck. French artillery farther inland joined the Kasba's guns. The *Dallas'* gun crews fired back as fast as they could. The destroyer *Kearny,* offshore, silenced one French 75-millimeter gun with brilliant long-range marksmanship. By miraculous luck, Brodie's ship did not suffer a single serious hit.

At 7:37 A.M. the *Dallas* came to a staggering halt. She was aground on a sandbar. But Brodie's mission had been accomplished. Against all odds, the *Dallas* had worked her way around the great bend, halfway down the far side of the U, to a place near the airport's seaplane ramp. The raiders piled into their rubber assault boats, paddled ashore and attacked the airport from the east. This was just the boost needed by the infantrymen north of the field—Company I of the 60th Infantry Regiment. Within half an hour their combined forces had cleared the French from the field. The carrier *Chenango* got ready to catapult its P-40s for the short flight to the airport. By the middle of the morning, Allied planes were using the shell-pocked runways.

Meanwhile, progress toward Casablanca had been

slow. The 3rd Division had advanced only to the northern outskirts of the sprawling city. Eisenhower was urging Patton to make up for lost time, pointing out that the fighting for Oran and Algiers was as good as over. Patton had told the troops to "grab the enemy by the nose and kick him in the pants." But it hadn't been quite that easy. There were still at least 3,600 French soldiers and 90 artillery pieces in the city. Furthermore, Harmon's medium tanks were in no position to help immediately; the head of the 2nd Armored's column was still fifty miles south of Casablanca. The French were capable of putting up a long, hard fight. In itself, this was a dreadful prospect. But a savage, costly battle might, in addition, make future coöperation between the French and the Americans hopeless.

All this time, the Allied command had been working hard to arrange a cease-fire. It was a tricky business, since it wasn't entirely clear whom, if anybody, the local French commanders would obey. Before dawn on the 11th, the 3rd Division men learned, to their relief, that they did not have to attack Casablanca after all. Admiral Jean Darlan, the Vichy Government's Minister of the Interior, was in Algiers, and he had ordered all the French forces in North Africa to break off hostilities at once. He was being obeyed.

General Mark Clark, an American, had conducted the negotiations, in which it was agreed that Darlan

19

and his associates would continue as the civilian administration in North Africa. The British and Americans hoped that the agreement meant the French would soon be fighting on the Allied side, but that was by no means certain. Darlan was bargaining for himself and all the Vichy officials in Morocco, Algeria, and Tunisia. There were, however, many Frenchmen, led by General Charles de Gaulle and his French government-in-exile in London, who regarded Darlan as a traitor for having worked with Germany. They were against any kind of arrangement with him.

But to Eisenhower, among others, the importance of moving east to the next battle took priority over every other factor. In just three days of fighting, the Americans had suffered 1,500 casualties, including more than 500 dead. And, of course, the Allies had also lost three days.

2
TUNISIA AND STALINGRAD

The race for Tunisia—and, in particular, for the ports of Tunis and Bizerte—began before the battles for Casablanca, Oran, and Algiers had ended. The Allied North African landings had caught Hitler and Mussolini, the dictators of Germany and Italy, by surprise. But they understood the threat, and reacted swiftly. The very next day, November 9th, German Stuka dive bombers and Italian Macchi 202 fighter planes from Sicily began landing in Tunisia. German Field Marshal Albert Kesselring, in Rome, ordered powerful reinforcements to get moving as fast as they could. These included first-rate German divisions from France and Germany, and Italian troops from Italy. The Tunisian ports were vital links in the lines supplying the German and Italian armies under General Erwin Rommel in northeast Africa. They had to be defended.

But Kesselring's problem had no satisfactory solution. He was forced to borrow air and sea transport from Rommel at a moment when Rommel couldn't afford to lend it. On November 4th his heavily armored forces had suffered a tremendous defeat at El Alamein, in Egypt. The leader of the victorious British forces was a comparatively new man on the scene— General Bernard Law Montgomery. Montgomery's offensive, originally designed to draw the attention of the German and Italian commanders away from the Northwest African landings, had begun on October 23rd. By brilliant planning and skillful maneuver, Montgomery had rammed his tanks right through Rommel's formations. The British had taken thousands of prisoners. The German-Italian threat to the Suez Canal was finally at an end. Withdrawing west along the Mediterranean coast of Africa, Rommel wanted to stop his retreat and make another stand— provided he got the supplies he needed. But by November 11th, while Kesselring was concentrating on the threat to Tunisia, Rommel had already been forced to retreat 200 miles. Montgomery was pursuing him as hard and as far as possible. The week's events —the British victory at El Alamein, and the landings on the northwest coast—threatened all the German and Italian positions in North Africa.

That, of course, was one of the Allies' main objectives. When the Allies held North Africa, they would control the Mediterranean Sea.

Hitler, the Allies' most powerful enemy in Europe, had not paid enough attention to the Mediterranean theater or to the strategic importance of British sea power. Now he saw their value, but he had even more serious problems to consider on the Russian Front. There, for the second summer in a row, he was directing a gigantic ground-and-air offensive, and the German advance had slowed to a crawl. The front lines stretched 1,200 miles, from Leningrad to the Caucasus Mountains. Hitler had 150 German, Rumanian and Finnish divisions in the battle, and the Russians had even more. For sheer geographical size, and the number of troops involved, it was the largest campaign in military history.

The Russian drive had begun, with Hitler confident and his generals nervous, sixteen months earlier, on June 22, 1941. Hitler had attacked Russia, breaking his nonaggression pact with Stalin, the Russian dictator. Hitler was convinced that his armies would encircle and destroy the Russian armies with lightning speed. He expected to defeat Russia in three months, and he had made no plans and provided no equipment for fighting through the winter.

At first, the Russians had been driven back with

terrible losses, but the Red Army was not destroyed. It had stopped the Germans on the outskirts of Moscow in December, 1941. Then a great Russian counteroffensive had thrown them back. The Germans had survived the Russian winter, and had attacked again in the spring of 1942, shifting the direction of their drive toward the south. Hitler was reaching for the prize objectives of his entire war effort: the Ukraine, with its wheat and coal, the Donets River basin, with its great industrial potential, and the rich Caucasus oil fields between the Black and Caspian seas. They were the economic substance for his mad dreams. With them, he thought, Germany and the Germans, as the master race, could dominate the world for at least 1,000 years to come.

It is hard to say for certain whether Hitler, at this point, was truly insane. Certainly he was having trouble facing facts when they were at odds with his wishes. He had stopped listening to his generals' advice, partly because they warned him against attempting the impossible. He had made himself commander of the armies in the field, a job for which he lacked the technical training. But despite his lack of military training, Hitler's 1942 offensive was close to success by autumn, when the Allies landed in North Africa. In Russia, German Army Group A had driven all the way to the Caucasus Mountains and was less than 400 miles from its final objective, the oil-production center of Baku.

Hitler, however, was unable to concentrate on this most important attack. He had become obsessed with taking the city of Stalingrad, which had comparatively little military significance. He had been squandering his forces, at Army Group A's expense, in the effort to dislodge the last Russian defenders from Stalingrad. And he had just fired General Franz Halder for warning him that Stalingrad was not worth the price. The Russians were clinging to four separate sections of the city on the west bank of the Volga River. Their supporting artillery was on the east bank. Their supplies and their wounded had to be ferried' across. Still they were hanging on, defending building by building with marvelous tenacity and skill.

Meanwhile, the Russians were building up for a counteroffensive on a huge scale. Stalin's armies were taking positions north and south of Stalingrad, where the German flanks were weak. The Russians were waiting for the ground to freeze; then their tanks could leave the roads and move cross-country. They were also waiting for the Allied landings to engage the Axis divisions in Africa, so Hitler could not use them for reinforcements.

Hitler continued to jam more and more German troops into the tight Stalingrad corner, inviting disaster. When the Russian preparations were called to his attention, Hitler flatly refused to admit that Stalin's troops—five powerful armies—existed at all.

Eisenhower hoped to win the race to Tunisia by speed, not strength, even though the Allied chances for doing so were slim. It was a long way from his nearest, or easternmost, toe hold at Algiers to Bizerte and Tunis: 560 miles by the truck route and 380 miles by air. And there was no way of knowing, from the tangled negotiations with the French, whether the French forces would help.

While supplies and reinforcements were still being unloaded, Eisenhower sent three groups of paratroopers east from Algiers to drop across the Tunisian border. Simultaneously he started a more powerful task force traveling overland to back them up. One battalion of the U.S. 509th Parachute Infantry dropped near Tebessa, and its patrols moved ahead toward Gafsa. British paratroopers landed at Bone and Souk El Arba. Contact with the German-Italian forces was made on November 17th. At Djebel Abiod, a little coastal town only forty miles from Bizerte, the British spearhead ran into an enemy reconnaissance column. The British held their positions, although they had the worst of the fighting that immediately developed. By the twenty-third of November, a clear-cut front line had been established. It ran south from just beyond Djebel Abiod to Bou Arada, and down the Eastern Dorsal mountain range to Gafsa. The southern two-thirds of the front was lightly held by patrols. The good news, however, was that the middle section of the line was manned by Frenchmen, ready to fight on the Allied side.

Still, the stabilization of an Allied front line there put an end to Eisenhower's hopes. Lieutenant General Kenneth A. N. Anderson, commanding the British First Army, stopped where he did because he couldn't advance any farther. General Walther Nehring, the German commander, was as determined to hold his Bizerte-Tunis bridgehead as the Allies were eager to snatch it away from him. His troops, though few in number, were mostly well-trained, aggressive para-troopers. By the end of November German and Italian strength in Tunisia had increased from 5,000 to 15,000 men. The winter rains had begun to turn the rugged terrain into an impassable sea of sandy mud. It was obvious that before the Allies could hope to take Bizerte and Tunis they would have to build up the size of their forces considerably.

This was a disappointment. Meanwhile, however, the Russians began their gigantic counteroffensive at Stalingrad. On November 19th, half a million Red Army soldiers with 1,500 tanks pushed forward in two great thrusts designed to encircle the city. These were the armies whose existence Hitler had refused to admit. Three days later the trap was closed. Inside it—an area about the size of Connecticut—the entire German Sixth Army of more than 260,000 soldiers was caught.

General Friedrich von Paulus, commanding the entrapped Germans, asked Hitler for permission to attempt to break out. He was refused. Hitler, as a general, could think of only one command: "Stand and fight to the last man." Militarily speaking, that made no more sense at Stalingrad than it did in Africa, where Rommel had received the same order. Both generals begged Hitler to let them withdraw, save as many of their divisions as they could, and thus be able to fight again on other battlefields.

Instead, an airlift was organized to supply Paulus' Sixth Army. And Field Marshal Hermann Goering, the grotesquely fat chief of the *Luftwaffe,* the German Air Force, promised to deliver 500 tons of supplies per day. (He actually delivered an average of 17 tons.) General Fritz Erich von Manstein tried to drive an armored column through the Russian ring, hoping to open a corridor for reinforcements, but he bogged down about halfway to Stalingrad. Paulus' situation grew worse every day. The Russians were trying, with all the strength they had, to squeeze the trap shut. Manstein told Paulus to try to break out: the two German forces were only thirty-five miles apart. Paulus hesitated. He couldn't bring himself to disobey Hitler's orders. Hitler modified his language: he said Paulus could break out, as long as he also held all his positions inside the ring. Since these commands were contradictory, Paulus struggled with his dilemma—

one of the most agonizing a commander has ever had to face. Meanwhile his chance of saving the Sixth Army evaporated. The Russians launched a new attack farther north, smashing their way through the Italian Eighth Army on the Don River and threatening Manstein's left flank. Most of the fantastically long German front began to unravel.

The Russians in the southeast attacked with a sudden fury. Hitler's Army Group A not only had to retreat from the Caucasus, but it narrowly avoided being cut off at Rostov. Hitler protested violently at every backward German step. By the end of January, 1943, the Russians had recaptured almost all the ground east of the Donets River except the Stalingrad pocket, now nearly 200 miles inside the Russian lines. Paulus' men were desperate. Epidemic sickness and brutal cold— for which, once again, they had no protection—were as devastating as the incessant Russian attacks.

Paulus asked Hitler for permission to surrender because it was inhuman to ask the German soldiers to suffer more. Hitler replied: "Capitulation is impossible. The Sixth Army will do its historic duty at Stalingrad until the last man in order to make possible the reconstruction of the Eastern Front."

Ten days later, on February 2nd, the Russians announced that all the Germans in the Stalingrad pocket had been killed or taken prisoner. The Stalingrad defeat had cost Hitler about 140,000 dead,

29

plus 90,000 prisoners—not to mention 60,000 vehicles, 1,500 tanks, and all the other equipment for 22 divisions. It was perhaps the most costly defeat in a single battle in German history.

3
GRAND STRATEGY

Allied strategy was made by the heads of three governments: Franklin Roosevelt, president of the United States, Winston Churchill, prime minister of Great Britain, and Josef Stalin, premier of the Soviet Union. The alliance, a matter of necessity, was far from a trusting one. Stalin was deeply suspicious of the democratic leaders, and vice versa. The differences between Great Britain and the United States were trivial by comparison.

From the moment Hitler attacked Russia, Stalin had appealed to Great Britain and the United States to open a second front in the West. He especially wanted them to invade the European continent. He insisted that the North African landings were not enough.

The Red Army was indeed pressed to its limits, and Roosevelt and Churchill could not let Russia lose. Yet, for the time being, a British-American landing in Europe would have no chance of success. Hitler was defending the coasts of France with surprising strength.

This had been proved by a tragic Canadian raid on Dieppe in August, 1942. Canada, like Australia and New Zealand and the other members of the far-flung British Commonwealth of Nations, was also fighting against the three Axis powers—Germany, Italy, and Japan. The Canadian commandos had had marvelous air support in their attack by fifty-six Royal Air Force fighter squadrons. But the 5,000-man raiding party had been mauled by the Germans. Three-quarters of the commandos had been killed, wounded, or taken prisoner. Also, the raid had cost the R.A.F. 106 planes, while only 48 German planes had been shot down.

The Dieppe failure was a sobering taste of what a major attack across the English Channel would encounter. But what really stopped the British and Americans from trying, early in 1943, was the Allied shortage of ships. They needed more of almost everything, especially assault vessels and landing craft. But shipyard construction and shipbuilding are slow processes; they could be hurried only so far.

The demands for ships of all kinds staggered the imagination of the Allied war planners.

There were already 1,000,000 Americans overseas, divided about equally between the European and Pacific theaters of the war. Merely supplying them, which was only one of half-a-dozen requirements, took millions of tons of freighter cargo space.

At the very outset the Allies had agreed that Hitler's defeat in Europe was to come before the all-out effort to beat the Japanese; but, even so, the Pacific war was demanding awesome numbers of men and tremendous quantities of materiel.

Stalin knew all about these problems in logistics. Still, he suspected that the North African campaign might be a substitute for, rather than a prelude to, an attack on Europe. He imagined that Great Britain and the United States might be stalling.

Roosevelt and Churchill, at the same time, were suspicious of Stalin. They were afraid that the Russians might make a separate peace with Hitler. The President and the Prime Minister could not forget that the Hitler-Stalin nonaggression pact of 1939 had allowed Hitler to invade Poland without fear of a Russian attack. Great Britain and France had been too far away to help their Polish ally.

Roosevelt and Churchill remembered all too well how Russia had occupied eastern Poland in 1939, acting in accordance with a secret postscript to the nonaggression agreement. They remembered how Stalin had stood by, and even sent supplies to Germany, while the German army marched into Denmark, Norway, the Netherlands, Belgium, Luxembourg, and France. The Russian dictator's only action, when Hitler was preparing to invade England in 1940, had been to annex the Baltic states of Estonia, Latvia, and Lithuania.

Great Britain's survival had been something of a miracle. She had not been invaded and had survived to fight another day, because her air force and navy had refused to give up control of the English Channel. They had stubbornly beaten off the Germans' fierce attacks. Hitler, however, had believed the English would realize they were as good as defeated. So he had turned his attention to the east and started a drive for Russia's wheat, coal, and oil.

All that was history by 1943, but Roosevelt and Churchill realized that their friendship with Stalin was not very old. Until Hitler had attacked Russia, Stalin's interest in British victory had been invisible.

Nonetheless, Roosevelt and Churchill looked ahead, not behind. Shortly before the African landings, Churchill had flown to Moscow to try to persuade Stalin that the North African landings, with the events that were planned to follow, constituted a second front—even though it was not the European second front Stalin wanted. Stalin had been impressed by

Churchill's fighting spirit, and Stalin was also quick to see how TORCH would indirectly assist the Red Army.

On the other hand, Stalin did not entirely appreciate how much Britain and the United States were doing by carrying the full weight of the all-important war at sea. Stalin admitted that he and his experts didn't understand naval strategy. They didn't even want to discuss it. In the atmosphere of mutual distrust perhaps that was just as well. Stalin might have been shocked to discover that the Western Allies, the two greatest naval powers in the world, had been losing the Battle of the Atlantic to German submarines, or U-boats.

For a year or more the German navy, commanded by Admiral Erich Raeder, had been appallingly successful at sinking Allied shipping everywhere, particularly between the United States and Great Britain. In 1942 alone, Allied ship losses had been more than 900 vessels, adding up to 6,250,000 gross tons. The rate of loss was higher than the rate of ship production of both countries combined. Not only were the Allies losing ships faster than they could build them but, so far, they had no answer to the brilliant tactics of the German submarine warfare chief, Admiral Karl Doenitz. Allied losses were increasing, not falling off.

It was a great crisis—a secret nightmare which Roosevelt, Churchill, and the Allied military men had to bear alone. The British and American publics knew nothing about it, and their leaders had no intention of telling Hitler more than he could guess from his own reports. But the situation was so grave that the Allies had to slow down the production of assault vessels and landing craft, badly as they were needed, to speed up cargo-ship production. President Roosevelt even had to slow down the American troop-training program. There was no point in getting divisions ready for battle before they could be shipped overseas and supplied.

Churchill, writing after the war was over, said: "The only thing that ever really frightened me during the war was the U-boat peril."

And Hitler, who needed something to be hopeful about, was beginning to think that Germany's undersea power would give him victory. He stepped up production of German submarines. In 1941 Doenitz had rarely had more than ten U-boats operating at once. By 1942 the number was usually more than 100. His submarine "wolfpacks" had made the Allied convoy runs to the Russian port of Murmansk nearly impossible. The difficulty of getting supplies to Russia was one part of the sea war Stalin was aware of. Since the Germans had submarine bases along the entire coast of Norway, they were able to strike with deadly effect at the slow-moving strings of Allied freighters.

One appalling example had been the ordeal of

Convoy PQ-17 in July, 1942. Thirty-three merchant ships, headed for Murmansk, had been given an unusually strong protective guard. Besides twenty-one escort vessels, the convoy was covered by three destroyers and four cruisers. Not far away, as a "distant support force," were two battleships, H.M.S. *Duke of York* and U.S.S. *Washington,* as well as three more cruisers and an aircraft carrier, the *Victorious.*

First the Germans had attacked from the air, as PQ-17, a few days out of Iceland, approached Bear Island in the Barents Sea. Despite the loss of four ships, the convoy maintained its disciplined formation. But then, because of a false intelligence warning that the German battleship *Tirpitz* was about to attack the convoy, PQ-17 was ordered to scatter. The various ships tried to reach Russian ports on their own. Such a dispersal was all that Doenitz's submarines needed. They sank twenty-one more Allied ships.

The key struggle against German submarines was taking place in mid-Atlantic. The vast central expanse of the ocean, beyond the range of Allied aircraft based in Newfoundland, Labrador, Iceland, and the British Isles, was known as "The Black Pit." Allied convoys in this area were at their most vulnerable. Doenitz, who had been getting thirty new U-boats a month, was concentrating his formidable strength on the Black Pit, making excellent use of his new submarine bases along the French coast.

This did not mean, however, that Allied ships were safe elsewhere. They had to be prepared for U-boat attacks almost everywhere. One day the raiders might strike at a convoy off Capetown, South Africa; the next day at coastal shipping in the Gulf of Mexico. Since ships traveling alone were the easiest targets, the Allies had been extending the convoy system as far as they could. But the shortage of escort vessels set a limit on how much could be done. And an inadequate convoy was in some ways worse than nothing. It became a bunched target without power enough to beat off an attack.

Doenitz' concentration on the Black Pit had been a blood-chilling success. The German score for the month of November, 1942, alone had been 807,000 gross tons of Allied ships sunk. December and January hadn't been quite as bad, but only because the U-boats had been ordered (too late) to try to disrupt the North African supply lines. It had to be assumed that Doenitz would return to the Black Pit and his November tactics of establishing two picket lines of waiting submarines, capable of attacking Allied convoys both coming and going. Allied submarine-warfare experts were wracking their brains, searching for answers to the Black Pit menace. But the terrible truth was that Allied leaders had no good reason to hope the German offensive would be less successful than before.

If the U-boats could resume sinking ships at the November rate, or anything like it, they would soon wreck all the British-American war plans.

In January, 1943, Roosevelt, Churchill, and their staffs met at Casablanca to sketch in the outlines for the future conduct of the war. Stalin did not attend. He explained that he was too busy with the war to leave Moscow. There was no arguing with him, but his absence did nothing to calm Western fears that he might be considering a separate peace with Hitler.

Both Roosevelt and Churchill appeared supremely optimistic—even though Russia's doubtful staying power and the awesome question of the sea war should have been enough to frighten them out of their wits. The two leaders agreed that "the defeat of the U-boat" would have—as it already had—first claim on their two nations' resources.

And, looking ahead to the total defeat of the Axis forces in North Africa, they agreed that the next British-American operation would be an invasion of Sicily.

Once the Allies were in possession of Sicily, Hitler would doubtless be forced to withdraw divisions from the Russian Front. For besides threatening Italy, the British and Americans would also be poised to attack the southern coast of France. Hitler would probably have to move troops down from northwestern France, as well. And there, the Allies were agreed, the cross-Channel attack would take place as soon as possible.

All that, of course, was looking very far into the future. More immediately, the Allied air offensive against Germany was beginning to tell. Roosevelt and Churchill agreed that the bombing should be stepped up. The United States Eighth Air Force, commanded by General Carl A. Spaatz, had begun to add its power to the raids the Royal Air Force had started two years earlier. The United States had 500 bombers in England, compared with the R.A.F.'s first-line bomber strength of about 800 planes. There had been steady improvement in the designs of both planes and bombs. Newer bombers could carry bigger loads of bombs, and the bombs themselves were more effective than before. Also, new radar devices had improved bombardiers' and navigators' accuracy.

The British and American air commanders could not agree, however, about a point of tactics. Americans were certain that precision bombing during the daylight hours would be more effective than the British nighttime raids against area targets. Both schools of thought were partly right.

The Eighth Air Force was equipped with B-17 Flying Fortresses suitable for daytime bombing, and General Spaatz was eager to prove the superiority of his methods. But, for the time being, he was frustrated because the Fortresses, despite their speed and the firepower of the ten 50-caliber machine guns they carried, were vulnerable to attack by German interceptor-fighter planes. U.S. fighters—the P-39s and P-40s—had a range of not more than 300 miles. Many of the most rewarding bombing targets were considerably farther away than 300 miles. This meant the bombers could not have a fighter escort.

Meanwhile, each bomber command was doing what it could and bombs were pounding German war plants around the clock.

The optimism Roosevelt and Churchill displayed at Casablanca was remarkable. Most Americans, like most Englishmen, were confident of ultimate victory, partly because they were so ignorant of the facts. For instance, no civilian in the United States had any idea that in the past year the Allies had lost 1,000,000 gross tons more than the total of new ships built. Scarcely anyone in either country, apart from the top-ranking military and political leaders, understood how close Hitler's 1942 summer offensive in Russia had come to victory. The men who met at Casablanca knew the truth and saw its implications. Nevertheless, without any qualms, they discussed the details of future victories almost as though the victories had already been won.

Behind their hopefulness, to be sure, there were great fundamental realities. For instance, the Allies possessed sixty percent of the world's industrial capacity, including eighty-six percent of its oil, and sixty-four percent of its iron. The haunting unanswered questions all involved transforming these basic strengths into weapons for immediate use.

In a year's time, the United States had raised thirty-seven new army divisions, and had almost doubled the number of men and women in uniform. Roosevelt reported to Churchill that the United States might be ready to send another 1,000,000 soldiers overseas in 1943—if, of course, the ships were ready to take them.

Besides being brave, the two Allied leaders were masters of propaganda. They wanted to express their own determination to win, and to stick with the job no matter what the cost. At the final press conference in Casablanca, Roosevelt's comment included a phrase that summed up this feeling. The President said:

Another point I think we have all had in our hearts and heads before, but I don't think it has ever been put down on paper by the Prime Minister and myself, and that is the determination that peace can come to the world only by the total elimination of German and Japanese war power.

Some of you Britishers know the old story—we had a general called U.S. Grant. . . . In my, and the Prime Minister's early days, he was called "Unconditional Surrender" Grant. The elimination of German, Japanese, and Italian war power means the unconditional surrender by Germany, Italy and Japan. That means a reasonable assurance of future world peace.

Churchill is said to have been surprised by this mention of "unconditional surrender"—which hadn't been discussed before in any detail—but he immediately agreed to what Roosevelt had said.

In any case, the phrase "unconditional surrender" became the best known product of the conference. Perhaps it did prolong the war, as Roosevelt's critics argued later, by making Italy, Germany, and Japan fight past the moments of their certain defeat. But it told Stalin that Great Britain and the United States were in the fight to the finish. It was an eloquent summary of the conviction which Roosevelt and Churchill shared: that the Allies simply had to triumph. And it told the Axis leaders in unmistakable language that they need not imagine there would be deals of any kind.

4
KASSERINE PASS

Although the Allied leaders at the Casablanca conference had full confidence in an eventual British-
American victory in North Africa, it had not yet been
won.

The Americans had brought enthusiasm and self-
confidence to the battlefield, and their good opinion
of themselves had been raised by the quick success of
the initial landings. But, like all green troops getting
their first taste of combat, the men had some bloody
lessons to learn.

February, 1943, was a time of morale-shaking United
States defeats.

In three months, Eisenhower's combat strength had
increased considerably. But his forces were no closer

to Tunis than they had been in November, and the front, running north and south, was nearly 250 miles long. The British held the northern part nearest the Mediterranean; the French were in the middle; and the United States II Corps, with Major General Lloyd R. Fredendall commanding, was on the south end. The terrain resembled parts of the American Southwest: desert, rocky mountains, with a few key roads, passes, valleys, and small, dusty towns.

Eisenhower hoped to launch an attack in the direction of Sfax as soon as he could get ready for it, possibly in March. But General Juergin von Arnim, who had replaced Nehring as the German commander in Tunisia, had no intention of letting Eisenhower call the shots. Von Arnim knew that in time the Allies would be able to achieve superior strength in Tunisia. Axis losses on the Russian front made that obvious. For the present, however, von Arnim was strong, and, as Rommel's veterans retreated under pressure from Montgomery's army, von Arnim became stronger. Besides their battle experience, Rommel's men brought with them quantities of armor—tanks, half-tracks, and self-propelled guns.

The Germans poked here and there at the long Allied front, and these limited attacks forced Eisenhower's subordinates to commit many of the reserves that had been earmarked for the Sfax offensive. The reserves had to be used to plug the numerous holes opened up by the Germans. On the last day in January, von Arnim captured Faid Pass from the French. The U.S. 1st Armored Division promptly tried to take it back, for the pass was an open door into the Allied positions. The Germans held fast. Then, on February 14th, von Arnim hit hard with his Fifth Panzer Army's 200 tanks. The Germans rolled through Faid Pass, spun off to the right and to the left, and quickly cut off several American units. Both shoulders of the Allied line were smashed. What had been a small gap became a big hole.

In the battle's confusion, Fredendall was slow to realize that this was a major attack. Tank for tank, American equipment was no match for the Germans'. Some of the enemy's anti-tank guns completely outclassed American weapons. Von Arnim's planes dominated the sky, and he used dive bombers and fighter bombers to support his ground forces with shattering effect. The 1st Armored had a terrible day, and its losses in men and equipment were heavy. But it was still optimistic, and prepared to counterattack the following day.

At the same time, following an earlier decision, II Corps got ready to pull out of Gafsa in the south. The plan was to concentrate American strength in the center. On the morning of February 16th, the 1st Armored's counterattack moved out, looking like a textbook model. A column of tank companies with tank-destroyer half-tracks on its wings advanced in the lead. Next came the self-propelled artillery, followed by the division's infantry, riding in half-track troop carriers.

But the Germans were ready and waiting. Instead of regaining ground, the 1st Armored lost more. That night II Corps tried to hold in front of a town called Sbeitla in the Western Dorsal Mountains. Some of the American troops were fighting in the dark for the first time. They got rattled and pulled out of position, throwing others into a panic. Soon the road was a vast traffic jam of out-of-control men and vehicles. Luckily, the 1st Armored's Combat Command B fought very well, and the Germans were unable to turn the American confusion into a rout.

But before the retreat halted, the II Corps had fallen back another twenty miles to Kasserine Pass, a three-mile gap in the next mountain range. The pass was only fifty miles from the main American base at Tebessa and not much farther, on the road branching off to the north, from the British base, Le Kef. The situation was getting desperate as the II Corps struggled to regain its balance. To make matters worse, Rommel's composite task force had pushed through Gafsa as the Americans withdrew. His battle-wise Africa Corps units threatened the southern flank of the U.S. forces.

When the Germans attacked Kasserine Pass on the

19th, the Americans were not ready. Their troops were strung across the entrance to the gateway, but they had not properly secured the high ground. Rommel's *Panzergrenadier* battalions seized the crucial heights, swept through the pass, and emerged into the flat valley beyond. In addition to its tanks and artillery, his powerful column included dual-purpose (antiaircraft or field gun) 88s, and a battery of rocket launchers. For the moment, it seemed practically unbeatable.

Then Rommel, whose great victories in the eastern desert had been won by concentrating his forces, made a mistake. The road forked. Tebessa, the American base, lay straight ahead. To the north, a right-hand turn, was the British base, Le Kef. Rommel should have chosen one objective or the other. Instead, he split his column and tried for both at once. Strong as they were, the German forces were not that powerful.

In front of Tebessa, at a minor pass called Djebel el Hamra, the 1st Armored's Combat Command B and a considerable part of General Terry Allen's 1st Infantry Division were waiting. February 21st and 22nd were suspense-filled days. During the intervening night, Rommel sent an enveloping force seven miles around to the south. But the U.S. 33rd Field Artillery Battalion's fire was brilliant. It, as much as anything else, forced the Germans to stop. American artillery was well placed, and Rommel's Stuka dive bombers were unable to silence the accurate 105-millimeter and anti-tank shooting. Toward the end of the afternoon, the 3rd Battalion of the 1st Division's 16th Infantry Regiment launched a strong counterattack. The Germans were driven off and forced into confused retreat. It was the first time in a week that the German offensive had suffered a major check.

At the same time, Rommel's northern attack had encountered a brigade of the British 6th Armored Division, with the artillery of the U.S. 9th Infantry Division, guarding Thala on the Le Kef road. The 10th Panzer Division approached deliberately. British Brigadier Charles Dunphie's tanks couldn't compete, head on, with Rommel's. So they used the parallel ridges in front of the town as protection for their lightly armored hulls. That maneuver succeeded until the German tankers, under Rommel's personal direction, fired down the terrain corridors from the side, or enfilade, positions. The British fell back as slowly as possible, squandering their tanks in the process. They were forced to retreat eight or nine miles to the last ridge in front of Thala before the furious battle ended for the day. In the process, Dunphie had used up almost everything he had.

In the middle of the night, the 9th Division artillery arrived. Its thirty-six howitzers, along with several batteries of 75-millimeter guns belonging to its infantry cannon companies, went into firing positions. They were very welcome. But Dunphie was still extremely short of infantry and tanks.

In an almost hopeless predicament, the British followed an ancient battlefield maxim: if you are too nearly beaten to defend, attack!

At first light, British tanks rolled forward in a brave counterattack. It got next to nowhere, and five more tanks were lost. The survivors of the ill-fated jab got back to their own lines and reported that at least seventy German tanks were waiting to move into Thala.

By sheer coincidence, however, the German intelligence officers had heard from local Arabs that the Allies were planning a major offensive through Thala. The aggressive spirit demonstrated by Dunphie's little tank attack seemed to confirm that idea. Rommel and the commander of the 10th Panzer Division now agreed that the Germans should stay put and wait for the big Allied counterpunch before continuing north.

The day passed. There was no Allied counterattack, of course. The British were merely hanging on. But the 9th Division artillery fired as fast as it dared, considering that it had only the ammunition it had brought along and didn't know when it would get more. American P-38s took off from an airfield that was practically all mud except for the steel-planked airstrip. Despite very low ceilings and poor visibility, they flew 114 sorties to the Thala area.

By hesitating—waiting for the imaginary Allied counterattack—Rommel had lost his chance.

Allied reinforcements began to arrive. By the 23rd, the British were in much better shape to hold Thala. The test never came, however, because Kesselring flew in from Rome and conferred with Rommel near Kasserine. The Germans agreed that they had better withdraw completely from western Tunisia and be content with having spoiled Eisenhower's offensive plans. Montgomery's British Eighth Army, by this time, was approaching the Mareth Line of old fortifications built by the French, facing the eastern approach to Tunisia. Kesselring hoped to attack the Eighth Army there, before Montgomery had organized his own assault.

Both the Americans and British near Kasserine were lucky that the Germans broke off the Thala engagement—lucky that Montgomery was forcing Kesselring to switch Rommel to the east. In just ten days the American losses had mounted to about 5,000 men. Only about 200 U.S. soldiers had been killed, but the wounded numbered more than 2,500. Almost an equal number of Americans had been taken prisoner.

These shocking figures were accompanied by the awareness, on the part of generals and privates alike, that the United States forces had made countless mistakes. Their intelligence work had been wretched. Their commanders had made an inexcusable blunder:

51

underestimating what the enemy might do. There had been acts of great bravery, but there had also been panic. Most of the failures could be laid to greenness. The Americans had not been properly trained and, at all levels, unit leaders were inexperienced.

The heavy losses in material things could be replaced. The big question was whether the Americans' shattered confidence in themselves could be regained.

5
THE MARETH LINE

Before the middle of March, the Axis forces in Tunisia twice more lashed out at the Allies. Their attacks were designed to throw the projected British-American offensive off balance.

First, von Arnim assaulted the British-held north end of the Allied line. He was beaten back, and lost a good deal of irreplaceable armor to no avail. Then Rommel struck at Montgomery's Eighth Army as it approached the Mareth Line, where the Italians and Germans planned their major defense. Montgomery's veteran gunners were brilliant. The British lost only six tanks and destroyed forty of the enemy's. Rommel lost the battle.

The most publicized of German war heroes was ill

and disheartened. Hitler had been paying no attention to Rommel's excellent suggestions. He resigned his command and headed for home, resuming the sick leave he had interrupted to fight the battle of El Alamein. His departure was kept secret, and for weeks Allied war correspondents continued to write about "Rommel's Africa Corps." German newspaper readers were no better informed. Hitler did not allow the news to be printed until May.

Rommel's career was by no means at an end, however. Montgomery, who had great respect for his generalship, would meet the German leader again.

At the same time, a change took place in the American command. Patton took over the U.S. II Corps from Fredendall. Patton had orders to revive the fighting spirit of the divisions in his Corps—the 1st, 9th, and 34th Infantry, and the 1st Armored. Within a day or two, II corps was indeed fighting mad. But the troops were mad at Patton, not the enemy.

Patton wanted to jolt his men into realizing that Kasserine was forgotten history. He also wanted to dramatize his high expectations for II Corps. He therefore ordered that all uniform regulations be enforced, including neckties in the front lines and steel helmets in the rear areas. While II Corps gasped with outrage, Patton himself drove around in his jeep bawling out violators and collecting fines—as high as fifty dollars for officers and twenty-five dollars for enlisted men.

But the General made his point. Every last man in the corps knew about the shift in the top command because its effect was felt down to the squad level.

And real rehabilitation had begun even before Patton assumed command. A school for soldiers was being run right in the face of the enemy. It involved reëquipment, reorganization, and the reëxamination of countless expensive battlefield lessons that had been learned. Camouflage was improved. All the men—not just combat engineers—studied mine detection and mine-field laying. Anti-tank gunners had been overawed by the toughness of the German tanks. Now they were taught how their small guns, skillfully emplaced, could destroy the enemy's heaviest armor by using the newest ammunition.

Eisenhower, worried about Patton's tendency to race around the battlefield like a junior officer, warned his subordinate: "I want you as a corps commander, not as a casualty."

Patton was not trying to win a popularity contest. He was determined that, next time, II Corps was going to win.

The test came quickly. But since there was still some question about the fighting ability of the American forces, II Corps had a limited assignment. Patton was to retake Gafsa, push through the mountains at El Guettar, and reconnoiter toward Maknassy and

Gabes—taking care, however, to avoid becoming too heavily engaged.

The idea was to threaten von Arnim's flank as a way of diverting Axis strength from the Mareth Line, where Montgomery would make the main attack.

The offensive began on March 17th with the American effort. General Terry Allen's 1st Infantry Division, reinforced by Colonel William O. Darby's 1st Ranger Battalion, walked almost unopposed into Gafsa. At the same time, Montgomery began sending exploratory patrols into the Mareth Line. Then the U.S. 1st Armored Division, plus one regiment of infantry from the 9th Division, fought its way into Sened and approached the Maknassy Pass. The 1st Division captured El Guettar, and pushed on.

Patton had reason to be pleased with II Corps. It was advancing in good style, and in perfect coördination with the British main effort. Darby's Rangers, especially adept at commando-style fighting, spearheaded the 1st Division's movement east toward Bou Hamran. Italian troops were holding the rugged ground at Djebel el Ank, a critical mountain pass. They were well dug in, and a head-on approach to their position would have been suicidal.

The Rangers were sent on a twelve-mile detour, a left hook around to the Italian rear over ground so rocky the Italians considered it impassable. Lieutenant Walter Jojic and the Ranger scouts studied the ground. For two dark nights in a row they crawled through the mountains, trying to find a path the battalion could follow. At nightfall, on March 21st, Darby led his men over Jojic's route. With their faces blacked with greasepaint, they scrambled over a series of rocky saddles, sometimes using toe holds and hand holds. The Rangers' months of speed-marching and physical conditioning proved their worth. Before dawn, most of the outfit had reached a rocky plateau above and behind the Italians' strong point.

The Rangers had no supporting heavy weapons, not even their mortars. They were armed with only their personal weapons: rifles, pistols, hand grenades, and bayonets. But they were experts at using speed and surprise, and well trained in the brutal techniques of close combat. The Italians had not heard them approaching. All the Italian weapons faced west, toward El Guettar.

As soon as it was light enough to see, the Rangers pounced. Screaming Indian battle cries, they bounded from rock to rock, leaping into Italian foxholes and machine-gun positions from behind. The first twenty minutes of bloody hand-to-hand fighting were decisive. Besides scores of Italian dead, the Rangers took more than 200 prisoners. By 8:30 A.M. the left shoulder of the pass was in American hands. Meanwhile, the 1st Division's 26th Infantry Regiment, with its supporting battalion of 105-millimeter artillery, was moving straight up the road, pouring shells into the Italian strong points on the right side of the pass. By noon, another 500 Italians had surrendered.

As the Americans planned, von Arnim was worried about this threat to his flank. He ordered his 10th Panzer Division, commanded by General Fritz von Broich, to stop Patton.

The British, meanwhile, were finding it exceedingly difficult to crack the main part of the Mareth Line, the twenty-mile section near the coast. But, farther inland, Montgomery's mobile New Zealand Corps had raced past the "impassable" west end of the fortified zone. A prodigious forty-eight-hour motor march over the edge of the desert had brought the corps to the El Hamma Pass. There an amazingly fast attack on Hill 201, a mesa in the middle of the gap, gave it control of a way into von Arnim's territory.

Montgomery immediately took advantage of this surprising development. Ordinarily he was a stickler for careful, detailed planning. Here, with brilliant decisiveness, he tossed aside his original plans, shifted the main power of his army far to the left, and transformed the New Zealanders' subsidiary thrust into the main British effort.

Now von Arnim needed his 10th Panzer Division to plug the El Hamma gap and stop the British, but it was already engaged. Von Broich had attacked

Terry Allen's 1st Division before dawn on March 23rd. The German line of advance followed the Gabes-Gafsa road, up the valley toward El Guettar. In the showdown between tank division and infantry division, the odds naturally favored the Germans. At the beginning, the battle seemed to be going entirely in von Broich's favor. The rising sun shone directly into the American artillery observers' eyes. Stuka dive bombers paved the way for the German tanks.

The German tanks and self-propelled guns, interspersed with infantrymen riding in armored carriers, rolled steadily up the valley in a formal hollow-square formation. From their positions in the flanking hills, the 1st Division men could see the main weight of the enemy's attack approaching. A long column of trucks loaded with more infantrymen followed until, at a designated point, the German soldiers leaped out and joined the mass of tanks and half-tracks. Following on foot, they used the hulls of the powerful vehicles as partial cover.

Then the German forces split into three prongs. One continued up the road, and the other two turned off toward the hills where the Americans were dug in. Despite the 1st Division's hail of fire, 10th Panzer kept moving. The German tanks overran the 32nd Field Artillery Battalion's position, knocking out its twelve howitzers. Part of the 5th Field Artillery Battalion was lost. There was savage hand-to-hand fighting as the huge tanks invaded the gun positions. But once their guns are out of action, gun crews are no match for armored tanks. The American casualties were very heavy.

Then one of the battle lessons the 1st Division had learned proved its value. The Americans had laid a crescent-shaped mine field across one likely tank approach, and it was covered by artillery as well as by the guns of two tank-destroyer battalions. Von Broich's tanks were temporarily halted by the mines. While they were stalled, the 1st Division brought all their fire power to bear on the German spearhead. The Germans fired back, but by the time the blazing exchange had ended, thirty of 10th Panzer's tanks were out of action. Mines had accounted for eight. American gunfire had stopped the other twenty-two.

Most important, the momentum of the German assault had been checked.

By nine o'clock, the tide of the battle had changed. The Germans pulled back, reorganized, and tried again in the middle of the afternoon. But the 1st Division, braced by the knowledge that the awe-inspiring German tanks really could be halted, was more than ready. The American artillery held its fire until the 10th Panzer tanks, closely followed by German infantrymen, were within easy range. Then they showered the enemy with air-bursts—shells with time fuses set to explode about fifteen feet in the air.

The jagged metal fragments showered down on the German foot soldiers with devastating effect. Patton was watching from a 1st Division observation post and, although he was proud of his gunners' proficiency, the slaughter made him shake his head with horror. "What a way to waste good infantry troops," he said.

The battle continued for two weeks. The Germans clung determinedly to their well-prepared positions, and von Broich's air support was excellent. II Corps was haunted by constant air raids—Stukas, ME-109s, Focke-Wulf 190s, and JU-87 twin-engined bombers— and slowed down by the enemy's skillful use of mines.

Besides their pie-shaped teller mines, which could blow up a jeep or knock the tracks off a tank, the Germans were using anti-personnel mines which the Americans called "Bouncing Bettys." There was nothing funny about them except their nickname. They were canisters filled with explosive and steel balls, triggered by little prongs. They were buried in the earth, with only the prongs sticking up. These were exceedingly hard to see. A man's weight was enough to set off the explosive. On detonation, the canister shot several feet in the air before it exploded. One or more of the steel balls was likely to hit anyone within fifty feet, with deadly effect. The psychological effect was bad too: the mines forced advancing soldiers to stop and look, and so move slowly.

Still, Patton's corps was carrying out its assignment

impressively. It had absorbed the full attention of von Arnim's mobile reserves, while Montgomery's Eighth Army poured through the El Hamma gap and ground its way north toward Tunis. By April 6th, the British were attacking the Germans and Italians at Wadi Akarit, seventeen miles north of Gabes. Here the Axis forces were making a new stand after their Mareth Line position had been outflanked.

Patton had been instructed to give the British as much help as he could. He ordered a special armored column, drawn mostly from the 1st Armored Division, to ram its way ahead without regard for casualties. It was called "The Benson Force" in honor of its commander, Colonel Clarence C. Benson. The entire II Corps was to follow its lead.

The Germans put on a tremendous artillery bombardment during the night of April 6th. Early the next morning the Benson Force—a battalion of tanks, a tank-destroyer company, and a company of armored infantry—started to advance. Patton watched them start, hounded Benson on the radio, and then jumped into a jeep and chased his spearhead force down the Gabes road. He found the tanks halted temporarily before a mine field. Forgetting Eisenhower's warning, Patton told his driver to go ahead—and luck was with him. The General led the way through the mines, and continued to lead the attack for a long way beyond them.

There was no necessity for Patton's dangerous heroics: Almost all the enemy forces had pulled out under cover of the night bombardment. The Germans were withdrawing into northeastern Tunisia for von Arnim's final stand.

The Benson Force kept rolling until, shortly after four o'clock that afternoon, it met a reconnaissance party from the British 2nd Armored Brigade. The Allied forces had linked up behind the retreating forces of the enemy—the First Italian Army, the German Africa Corps, and the Fifth Panzer Army.

6

TUNIS AND BIZERTE

The Axis forces were pulled together into a compact bridgehead at the northeastern tip of Tunisia, prepared to fight as long as they could to forestall a final Allied victory. At the end of the second week in April, the front lines were a great arc. It curved from a point east of Cape Serrat on the Mediterranean Sea to Enfidaville on the Gulf of Hammamet, about thirty miles from Bizerte and Tunis, the main Allied objectives.

The British—General Alexander and his staff, in particular—still doubted II Corps' fighting ability. They felt that the greenest of the American divisions, the 34th Infantry, should be pulled out of the line and sent back to a rear area for further training.

But Eisenhower insisted that II Corps remain a unit. And he put a good deal of pressure on Alexander to agree that II Corps be assigned more than a minor role in the final offensive drive.

II Corps had the northern section of the line. Its front was some thirty-six miles wide. Of all the Allied corps, it was closest to Bizerte. If everything went well, II Corps should be in at the finish, and win a full share of the victory.

The time had come for Patton, who was to command the U.S. Seventh Army for the Sicilian invasion, to leave II Corps. His successor was General Omar N. Bradley, a soft-spoken, deliberate man. Compared with Patton, Bradley seemed about as colorful as a G.I. boot. He had been Deputy Corps Commander of II Corps since shortly after the fight for Kasserine Pass and he was well aware of all the American divisions' strengths and weaknesses. He was convinced that the 34th Division was no better and no worse than the others. What it needed above all, Bradley felt, was the self-confidence that comes from victory in battle.

"Give me the division," Bradley told Alexander, "and I'll promise you they take and hold their very first objective." Then, characteristically, he made that boast sound a little less preposterous: "They'll take it if I have to support them with every gun in the corps."

Alexander laughed. "Take them," he said. "They're yours."

Montgomery's Eighth Army led off with a night attack near Enfidaville on April 19th. He was trying to fool the Germans and Italians into thinking it was the main Allied effort. He found out immediately that the enemy had lost none of its determination; indeed, Axis reinforcements were still being flown into Tunisia from Sicily at a rate of more than 1,000 a day. The Eighth Army gained very little ground, and the British casualties were heavy. Montgomery stopped after two days to reorganize and shift the main weight of his attack.

Then, just as Anderson's British First Army was on the point of making its real main effort near Medjez el Bab, the German Hermann Goering Division beat it to the punch. The enemy attack surprised the British. The Germans gained about five miles along a twelve-mile section of the line. Within a matter of hours, they were beaten back, but von Arnim now knew what he had only guessed before. Anderson was obviously preparing for an offensive to start within the next day or two.

For four days, starting on April 22nd, Anderson's divisions inched forward. They had lost the element of surprise, and the Germans had done a masterful job of blocking the mountain passes with mines. They had also put strong detachments on all the dominating hills. Only at one point, near Pont-du-Fahs, could Anderson's tanks break through the German defenses.

Von Arnim quickly moved to patch up the break, and the German 10th Panzer Division was locked in a savage struggle with the British 6th Armored Division. The losses on both sides were frightful, and the British were unable to make any appreciable advance.

Meanwhile, farther north, Bradley's II Corps was doing considerably better, thanks in part to the enemy's concentration of strength opposite Anderson. The Americans hoped to use the Tine River Valley—almost ideal tank terrain—for an approach to the town of Mateur and, ultimately, Bizerte. First, however, the Germans would have to be driven off the hills and ridges along the valley.

The attack started briskly on Good Friday, April 23rd. The 1st Division's three regimental combat teams moved ahead over the tough, mountainous ground. But, by the end of the third day, two facts were evident: the enemy was going to put up a tremendous fight, and the 1st Division's progress depended on somebody's taking the tallest of all the hills. Hill 609—so-called because that was its height in meters on the French maps—was 200 feet higher than any other peak near it, and a marvelous observation post. From its summit, the Germans were raking the 1st Division with stunningly accurate artillery and mortar fire.

Although Hill 609 was well to the left of the 1st Division's projected path of advance, Bradley decided to put the 34th Division into the line beside the 1st Division, and make Hill 609 its first objective. General Charles W. Ryder, commanding the 34th, knew the job was rugged. The German defenses were skillfully prepared.

For three days Ryder tried one maneuver after another, but Hill 609 seemed almost unapproachable. Smaller hills around it dominated the low ground, just as Hill 609 dominated the north flank of the Tine River Valley. Patrols advanced comparatively easily, but when Ryder tried to move larger units over the same routes, they drew a hail of deadly German fire. Infantrymen who worked their way to high ground were pinned down by heavy machine-gun fire from the nearby heights. Then, before the Americans could organize a position, the Germans invariably counter-attacked.

By April 30th, the bloody, seesawing struggle for possession of the lesser hills had cost II Corps nearly 2,500 casualties. And Hill 609 was still firmly in German hands. It began to look as if Bradley's faith in the 34th Division had been wrong.

But the Germans were showing some signs that their losses had been heavy, too. Starting early in the morning of the 30th, both the 34th and the 1st attacked again. By occupying the enemy's attention, the 1st Division gave Ryder's 34th strong support. And, as he had promised, Bradley had massed as much of the corps' artillery as he could in support of Ryder's effort.

Bradley had also given Ryder a company of seventeen Sherman tanks that belonged to the 1st Armored Regiment. It was a surprising idea; tanks are not ordinarily used to assault a mountain. Captain Robert D. Gwin, the tank company commander, had made his own reconnaissance and had worked out his own tactical plan the night before. He intended to use the Shermans as self-propelled artillery.

Gwin's tanks rolled toward Hill 609 from the flank and rear. Because of their armor, their crews could ignore the German machine-gun and mortar fire. They slammed one 75-millimeter shell after another into the enemy's strong points. This was just what the 34th Division infantrymen needed.

The 3rd Battalion of the 135th Regiment was the first to get a patrol to the summit of Hill 609. There was time enough to organize against the inevitable enemy counterattacks, and now it was the Americans who had the advantage of a superb observation post. By the afternoon of the following day, the 34th Division had captured not only Hill 609 but all the important ground around its base.

The 34th Division had distinguished itself. From that day on, the men of the 34th considered themselves members of a great outfit. There was no stopping them. Bradley had gained much more than an important hill. He had acquired what amounted to a new, first-rate division.

Once Hill 609 was in American hands, the 1st Division could resume its advance, opening up the Tine River Valley. General Ernest Harmon's 1st Armored Division tanks roared down it, headed for Mateur. By May 3rd, the 1st Armored had the city under its control.

Meanwhile, General Manton Eddy's 9th Infantry Division was making progress on the north end of the American line, moving through difficult ground that earlier had given the British considerable trouble. The U.S. II Corps was now leading the entire Allied attack.

Anderson's main effort in the Allied center got under way with a tremendous artillery preparation. On May 6th, General Carl A. Spaatz, now commanding the Northwest African air forces, sent every plane he had into the air for a day-long Allied strike. It was the most devastating air attack of the whole campaign. More than 2,000 bomber, fighter-bomber, and strafing missions were flown, concentrating on a target area only 6,000 yards wide. Anderson's tanks pounded their way forward. By nightfall, the tip of the armored spearhead reached Massicault on the road to Tunis.

The battered German and Italian divisions fell back, as determined as ever to make a stand if they could find a place to do so.

Harmon's tanks pushed beyond Mateur toward Prot-
ville to the east and Ferryville, on Lake of Bizerte, to
the northeast. The 34th Division slogged ahead in the
direction of Chouigui. The 1st Division, meanwhile,
made a costly mistake. On this drive the division had
been instructed not to overtax itself. It had been
carrying a great share of the fighting so far and its
casualties approached 4,000 men out of its total strength
of only 17,000.

But General Allen, instead of merely applying pressure to the enemy forces on the 1st Division front,
attempted an ambitious attack into the foothills east
of the Tine River. He may have believed that the
Axis forces were practically demoralized. He was
mistaken. The crack German regiment there was
made up of Luftwaffe volunteers converted to infantrymen, and was the outfit that had defended Hill 609
so long and well. It hit back hard, with no visible signs
that von Arnim knew he was beaten. The 1st Division
had to retreat. Allen was lucky that his losses, which
were heavy, were not worse.

Eddy's 9th Infantry Division drove for Djebel
Cheniti, the Germans' last tenable defensive position
west of Bizerte. Here the American force outmaneuv-
ered the enemy beautifully. As soon as the 9th
Division had possession of the hill that dominated the
battlefield, there was little more the Germans could do.

Victory came with a sudden rush. On May 7th,

while the British crashed through into Tunis, the 9th Division's half-tracks entered Bizerte and clanked through the city's rubble-filled streets. The two events, forty miles apart, took place within a single hour. It took another six days for the Allies to seize Cape Bon, but the delay was caused by the physical difficulty of accepting the unconditional surrender of the huge German-Italian force—some 275,000 soldiers, including the remnants of the Africa Corps.

The campaign had taken seven months, but by May 13th the Allied victory in Tunisia was complete.

Many of the Italian prisoners seemed well enough satisfied to be out of the war. The Germans were somewhat less philosophical about defeat. But they believed their losing fight had won time for the Reich to gain strength. This was an echo of Hitler's own mistaken idea. Hitler, who had sacrificed a whole army to no good purpose, felt he had delayed the Allied invasion of Europe. Therefore he believed that the price had not been too high. But the truth was that the Axis no longer had a suitable force ready and available to defend the Continent.

No one could tell Hitler that his judgment was incredibly wrong. Among the many other factors he was evaluating incorrectly was the ability of the United States fighting forces. Green troops had become battle-tested veterans. The units that composed II Corps had shown a remarkable ability to learn, and correct mistakes, in the middle of combat. Enlisted men and officers alike were prepared for the battles that lay ahead.

The Allied shipping shortages, more than anything else, had been delaying the British and Americans. The victory in Tunisia, by reopening the Mediterranean to Allied ships, was worth perhaps 1,000,000 tons of shipping. The campaign had also taught the British and the Americans to fight together, despite the many natural causes for friction. And a French army, though small, had been reborn. It had fought on the Allied side for France's ultimate liberation.

THE WAR IN SICILY AND ITALY

U.S. paratroopers adjust packs and parachutes before boarding their C-47 for the drop in Sicily. The American flags on their arms are for identification purposes. *(U.S. Air Force)*

General George S. Patton, Jr., commander of the U.S. Seventh Army at Sicily. *(U.S. Army)*

Infantrymen advance along
Sicilian cliff near Capo Calava
(U.S. Army)

During German strafing of the Salerno landing, members of a
beach battalion hug the ground. *(UPI)*

New Zealand soldiers in Cassino on the day after its capture
by Allied forces examine a wrecked tank. *(Wide World)*

Amphibious "Ducks" ferry supplies to the beachhead at Anzio.
(Wide World)

7
SICILY

D-Day for the invasion of Sicily was July 10, 1943. H-Hour was 2:45 A.M., when the quarter moon would set. The full weight of a nine-division (four American, five British) assault was aimed at Sicily's southeastern corner. Twenty-four hours before the attack, when it was almost impossible to halt the gigantic 3,200-ship invasion fleet, the wind began to blow. Gales of forty miles an hour whipped the water. It looked as if the preliminary airdrop and glider landings by the U.S. 82nd Airborne Division and the British 1st Airborne Division would have to be canceled. The seaborne landings seemed doubtful, too. High waves would ruin them.

But at the last moment—the early evening of D-

Minus-One—the storm suddenly slackened. The attack proceeded as planned.

The paratroopers, who went first, had some trouble with the weather, and more trouble with the complex pattern of their approach flights. To the east, 133 huge motorless gliders towed by C-47 transport planes were cut loose far from their mark—a bridge over a canal south of Syracuse. Montgomery had wanted to keep the bridge intact. There were 1,600 British paratroopers aboard. Many were lost when their gliders splashed into the dark sea. Only twelve of the aircraft landed near the bridge, and only a handful of men—eight officers and sixty-five enlisted men— managed to work their way to the objective. This force took possession of the bridge and prepared to defend it. A German battalion counterattacked. The English held. But as D-Day passed the paratroopers were hit, one by one. By late afternoon only nineteen of them were still on their feet, and the Germans drove them away from the bridge. But before the enemy could blow up the bridge, infantrymen from Montgomery's Eighth Army, who had landed on the beaches, arrived. They retook the bridge and rescued the surviving paratroopers.

Farther west, behind the American beaches, General Matthew B. Ridgway's four battalions of paratroopers also had a bad time. Instead of landing bunched near Gela, the 1st Infantry Division's objective, they were

scattered for sixty miles—the full length of the invasion coast on the American side. Many of the men
couldn't figure out where they were. Since they
couldn't perform their assigned missions, they did
whatever damage they could: blowing bridges, cutting
telephone lines, and attacking groups of enemy soldiers
wherever they found them.

General Albert Guzzoni was commanding the German and Italian forces on Sicily. His headquarters
had already made the mistake of thinking the bad
weather would make invasion impossible. Now they
were completely baffled by the 82nd Airborne's drop
pattern—and no wonder! By creating confusion and
inflicting random damage behind enemy lines, the
U.S. paratroopers had speeded up the American
advance by perhaps forty-eight hours, according to
Patton's estimate.

By the time the sun rose, the Allied landings were
all making good progress. Guzzoni's defending army
was strong. He had two first-class German divisions
and nine good Italian divisions on an island not much
larger than the State of Vermont. There were thirty-
two military airfields, and countless concrete and
barbed wire defensive strong points. But the coast was
being defended by inferior static divisions, filled
with Sicilian reservists—local men and boys who were
untrained, unwilling draftees. Guzzoni and his commanding officer, Kesselring, could only hope they

would be able to delay the Allies long enough for the Axis to mount a powerful armored counterattack.

On the American left, General Lucian K. Truscott's 3rd Infantry Division had gotten ashore with remarkable ease in several brand-new kinds of beaching craft. There were large LSTs (Landing Ship, Tank), LCIs (Landing Craft, Infantry), and LCTs (Landing Craft, Tank). All had bows that opened like great doors and ramps that lowered to the beach. Men, vehicles, and equipment could be put ashore directly instead of having to transfer to smaller boats. In the center of the American sector, the 1st Division had landed in front of Gela, pushing the perimeter of its beachhead inland. On the right, General Troy Middleton's 45th Infantry Division, in combat for the first time, had landed skillfully near Scoglitti. Another new invention, the floating two-and-a-half ton trucks called "Ducks" (from a meaningless factory designation, DUKW), had proved as successful as the new beaching craft.

Guzzoni had promptly ordered two of his best divisions, the Goering Panzer and the Livorno, to counterattack down the Gela road toward the 1st Division beaches. The enemy's sixty Mark IV tanks took some time to move to the battlefield. When they got there on the morning of the second day, Allen's artillery and anti-tank guns were still being unloaded. The outpost line was held by infantrymen. The only weapons they had that were capable of stopping a tank were a few rifle grenade-launchers and bazookas. On the other hand, the 1st Division had been through a great deal of fighting. The veterans' battle experience, coupled with great courage, stood them in good stead.

Incredible as it seems, there is nothing a tank can do to a man crouched in the bottom of a properly dug foxhole—not even if it runs right over him. The battle-tested infantrymen knew this. They did not let the roar and fury of the German tanks throw them into panic. They did not abandon their foxholes. They stayed put. Then, after the tanks had rolled past, the infantrymen stood up and fired at the German soldiers who were following close behind.

Meanwhile, Allen was rushing every possible gun to the danger points. The 1st Division was perilously short of its own artillery, but the navy had fire-support teams ashore with radios. The 1st Division called for help.

For ten suspense-filled hours, two cruisers and eight different destroyers offshore fired salvo after salvo onto the Gela plain. The fire-support parties, like artillery forward observers, made corrections by radio. The navy's shooting was marvelous. Though the great German tanks weighed twenty-six tons, a cruiser's shell could split one open like a melon.

Guzzoni's counterattack failed—even though the German column got within 2,000 yards of the cluttered beach. When the enemy withdrew at the end of the day, thirty German tanks—half the total number—were left smashed and burning on the field.

Before there was time to celebrate, a terrible mistake occurred. Another contingent of Ridgway's paratroopers—2,000 men in 144 planes—was coming in as midnight approached. They hoped to seize the Farello airfield, just east of Gela, and thus assist the 1st Division. Warning messages had gone out to the invasion fleet and the antiaircraft batteries ashore to look out for friendly troops. But there hadn't been quite time enough for everyone to understand. Also, swarms of German planes had been over the beaches both days. Understandably the American antiaircraft gunners were slightly trigger-happy. And Ridgway's C-47s came in, directly over the Allied ships and the battle zone, on the heels of a big German air raid. The U.S. planes were flying at drop height, a mere 700 feet.

One of the U.S. naval guns opened fire. Tracer bullets streaked up into the sky. Seconds later, the whole sky was ablaze, as countless other guns followed suit. The slow-moving transport planes were easy targets, and twenty-three of them were shot down in a very short time. About 100 of the 82nd's officers and men were killed. The large number of wounded brought the total number of casualties up to about 400.

With the failure of his Gela counterattack, Guzzoni

pulled back, trying to build up defenses in the Catania area. Such a strategy was his best hope of blocking Montgomery's route up Sicily's eastern coastline to Messina. The enemy's possession of Mount Etna, 10,705 feet high, gave the Germans and Italians an advantage. That old volcano and the mountainous terrain around it dominated the entire northeastern section of Sicily.

At first the British advanced swiftly. The city of Syracuse was in Montgomery's hands before dawn on D-Plus-One. But from there on, as the Eighth Army approached Catania, enemy resistance grew more and more stubborn.

On the American side, Patton's Seventh Army began to expand its initial foothold on the coast. Its prisoner-of-war cages filled up at an almost embarrassingly fast rate. Most of the Sicilian reservists had no interest in fighting with their German allies, and thousands of Italian soldiers felt the same way. The U.S. 1st Division was in control of Gela and the Farello airfield. The 45th Division took its objectives, including the Cosimo airfield, so quickly that the infantrymen captured twenty-six enemy planes on the ground. Shortly afterward, a German pilot, flying a Junkers 88 twin-engined bomber, came in for a landing. To his astonishment, antiaircraft guns around the field fired on him. He landed safely, got out of his plane, and started to scold everybody in sight for their mistake.

It was then, and only then, that he realized the field was in Allied hands.

By July 17th, the 3rd Division had captured Agrigento, another port. Good as the American beach-landing system was, a port with docks would be a valuable addition to the Allied supply system. From there on, the American advance toward Palermo was spectacular. The 3rd Division moved 100 miles up the coast in four days—a speed record that would have been good for a march on a maneuver. Truscott's men had to take time for a number of tough fights on the way, however.

The 82nd Airborne, now fighting on the ground, and the 2nd Armored Division kept pace with the 3rd. The 45th Division, which had been shifted to the left of the 1st Division, fought its way up the middle of the island, through Caltanisetta. Middleton's regimental combat teams leapfrogged up this principal road, fighting an amazing six-day battle without ever stopping to rest. General Bradley saw a letter written by a German soldier to his brother on the Russian front: "These astonishing Americans," it said. "They fight all day, attack all night, and shoot all the time."

Palermo, the capital of Sicily, fell on July 22nd. The streets were cluttered with rubble when Patton arrived to look over the city the following day. The 82nd Airborne took the northwestern tip of the island, adding 20,000 more Italian prisoners to the total bag.

The 45th Division reached the northern seacoast, near Isnello, at the same time. In the 1st Division sector, where the Germans and Italians were resisting most determinedly, Allen's men advanced from Enna to Petralia.

All this time, Montgomery, fighting against the best of Guzzoni's forces, was having trouble on the eastern coast. The Germans had held the British south of Catania. Montgomery had attempted to swing his 1st Canadian Division far around to the left, by-passing the difficulty. But the Canadians had proceeded only as far as Leonforte, just northeast of Enna.

Since Patton had almost completed his original assignment, Eisenhower, through his deputy, Alexander, gave the Seventh Army new orders. Patton was to attack toward Messina, a 90-degree turn to the east, and help the British capture the city.

Meanwhile, on the mainland of Italy, a significant political drama was taking place. On July 19th, Rome had been stunned by the first air raid it had suffered. A tremendous Allied attack by 500 Liberators and Flying Fortresses had pulverized the railroad yards and damaged the airport. Mussolini was conferring at the time with Hitler at Feltre in northern Italy. It was the thirteenth such meeting between the two dictators. Mussolini wanted more German military help, but all he got was a fantastic oratorical performance. Hitler spoke for three solid hours before lunch, and almost that long again afterward. The Fuehrer was trying to inspire his Italian partner with a fierce will to resist, the way the Russians had resisted at Stalingrad.

Mussolini said practically nothing. He was disheartened. The Italians were as discontented with his leadership as they were with their country's alliance with Germany. They were distressed by the Allied successes in Sicily, or as much as they knew of them.

On the night of July 24th, the Fascist Grand Council, a body of men appointed by Mussolini himself, assembled for the first time in four years. Mussolini was forced to listen to violent criticism from his own appointees. This was a fantastic turnabout for the ruthless tyrant who had been in power for more than twenty years. And before the meeting adjourned, the Grand Council had voted Mussolini out as commander in chief of the Italian armed forces. The figurehead king of Italy, Victor Emmanuel III, was to replace him. The Italian dictator had fallen!

At the King's request, 71-year-old Marshal Pietro Badoglio formed a new government. Mussolini's Fascist party was dissolved, and most of his henchmen were expelled from government jobs. The Romans, and Italians everywhere, rioted with joy.

Hitler correctly assumed that Badoglio would soon try to negotiate for peace. The Fuehrer's solution was to attempt a counter-coup to put Mussolini back in power. But he was overlooking the fact that Mussolini had become perhaps the most hated man in Italy.

The new government had placed Mussolini under arrest and confined him in a jail on the island of Ponza. It planned to move him around from place to place to forestall any attempt, by Mussolini or anyone else, to arrange a comeback.

The Allied advance continued in Sicily. The 45th and 3rd divisions were on the extreme left flank, along the coast. The 1st Division turned right and fought into Nicosia and on toward Troina. The British closed in on Adrona, immediately south of Mount Etna. As the semicircular front moved northeast, toward Messina, Guzzoni knew Sicily was lost. He was fighting for time. He wanted to save as many German and Italian divisions as he could by ferrying them across the Strait of Messina to the toe of Italy. The Germans bore the brunt of the delaying action. Once again they showed that, given mountain terrain favorable to defense, they were masters at mining, road-blocking and, above all, the swift, concentrated counterattack.

As the 1st Division approached Troina, a fortress-like town on the top of a mountain, it was confronted by a huge, almost treeless, bowl-shaped depression in the ground. Allen's leading troops, with some men from the 9th Infantry Division, advanced boldly into the hollow. The German 15th Panzer Division counterattacked, forcing the Americans back.

The battle raged on, becoming one of the most fiercely fought actions of the entire war. Throughout the first week in August, the Americans tried to out-flank Troina. They attempted to cut the Germans' exit roads leading down from the far side of the mountain. The Allies, by now, had more powerful artillery and overwhelming superiority in the air. But the 15th Panzer's observation posts were exceedingly good, and what they lacked in numbers of guns they made up in accurate shooting. Troina was rocked by 500-pound aerial bombs. Still the Germans held out, and every Allied advance was answered by a German counter-attack—a fantastic total of twenty-four in the course of a week.

Finally, on the sixth of August, the 16th Infantry Regiment climbed the mountain and entered Troina. Although it was an important victory, it was primarily an enemy concession. The Italians had started to es-cape from Sicily on the 3rd. The Germans were get-ting ready to follow them.

Patton and Montgomery closed in, doing their best to prevent the enemy forces from getting away. The Americans tried three different amphibious landings, jumping ahead along the north coast in order to cut off some of the retreating enemy units. Many German and Italian prisoners were taken, but not enough to justify the casualties the Americans suffered.

On August 10th, when the Allied pressure was nearing its peak, General Patton was on his way to talk to Bradley, his II Corps commander. He stopped to inspect the 93rd Evacuation Hospital. He talked to many of the men who had just been wounded, trying to make them feel better. Then he came to two men who hadn't been wounded. One had a high fever. The other was a battle-fatigue case. His nervous system had not been able to stand the strain of what he had endured.

When the soldier said something about there being nothing wrong with him except his nerves, Patton flew into a tantrum. He slapped the side of the soldier's helmet-liner, and knocked it to the ground. He ranted around the hospital, creating a tremendous rumpus, shouting threats, and embarrassing the doctors, nurses, and staff.

News of the incident got back to the United States and created a public furor. Many people thought Patton should be dismissed. Eisenhower and Bradley, who knew the General well, understood that the affair was an unfortunate example of his swaggering, show-off style gone wrong. Patton knew from experience that men could sometimes be shocked into acting more bravely than they felt. His grave mistake was to behave in a hospital like a platoon commander on the battlefield. Patton later apologized to everyone concerned in the unfortunate incident. He was Eisenhower's outstanding expert in tank warfare and, on the record, the U.S. Army's best ground gainer. Eisenhower had no replacement for him. The commander in chief did his best, though Patton continued to suffer for his mistake, to keep his punishment from growing out of all proportion to his misconduct.

On August 17th, long before the repercussions of the "slapping" incident reached their climax, the British and Americans occupied Messina. A 3rd Division platoon, with a 45th Division patrol accompanying it, walked from the city's outskirts to the City Hall without meeting any resistance. Minutes later, a British lieutenant colonel arrived on the scene, and announced that Montgomery's advanced units were not far behind. The Allied triumph was only partial: the enemy had made good its escape to Italy. Some 100,000 German and Italian soldiers, 10,000 vehicles, and 50 tanks had been ferried across the Strait of Messina during the previous two weeks.

Still, possession of Sicily was a great gain, and the 150,000 Axis casualties (compared with 31,000 for the British and Americans) seriously weakened the enemy. Most of these casualties were Italian. The defeat had knocked Italy almost completely out of the war.

8
ITALY

Scarcely more than two weeks later, on September 3rd—exactly four years after the war had begun—the Allies invaded the Italian mainland. Under cover of darkness Montgomery slipped two divisions, the Canadian 1st and the British 5th, across the Strait of Messina. They met practically no resistance, and began to push cautiously up the toe of the Italian boot.

On that same day, the Badoglio government secretly signed Italy's surrender. It was not to be announced until September 8th because the Italians were terrified of German reprisals. Badoglio and his supporters hoped that the Allies would invade with a force big enough to protect Italy from the Germans. But since there were sixteen German divisions already in Italy

—not to mention thousands of German agents planted in the Italian government—that was more than the Allies could do.

Montgomery's quick landing, which secured the Strait of Messina, was also designed to distract the Germans' attention from the main Allied assault. This came six days later at Salerno, south of Naples. After a tremendous air and naval bombardment, General Mark Clark's Fifth Army, made up of one British and one American corps, stormed ashore at four different places on the crescent-shaped shore of the Bay of Salerno. The date was September 9th, and the Germans—not to mention the entire world—were reacting to the Italian surrender announcement. Most of the German divisions near Naples were busy disarming Italian troops in order to prevent their fighting on the Allied side. Even so, one first-class German division, the 16th Panzer, was ready and waiting to defend Salerno Bay.

Clark's men met stiff resistance on the beaches, especially on the extreme right, where enemy fire was fierce. There the untried U.S. 36th Infantry Division landed without any preliminary bombardment. The tactical planners thought that surprise would more than make up for the lack of advance shelling. They were wrong. The 36th Division's casualties were heavy in the first few hours. Nevertheless, the men got ashore and moved on into the mountainous ground behind the beaches.

By the end of D-Day at Salerno, all the Fifth Army landings had succeeded. The 36th, however, hadn't quite reached the summit of one hill that it needed. Also, there were four small, separate beachheads instead of one long front. But luckily the 16th Panzer could not take advantage of the temporary gaps. On the extreme left, at Maiori, Colonel Darby's Ranger battalion had surprised and overwhelmed a German armored reconnaissance company and was in fine shape. The Rangers were six miles inland, dug in on the high ridges overlooking the Naples plain. They were ready to raise havoc with the enemy's communications between Naples and Salerno. As for the town of Salerno itself, British commandos—the models for Darby's marvelous outfit—had taken and held it.

For the moment the situation seemed good. But in striking for Salerno Bay, Eisenhower had reached as far up the western coast of Italy as his fighter support would allow. His air bases were all in Sicily, too far away for Allied fighters to stay over the battlefield for more than fifteen minutes.

For that reason, the Allies were eager to capture the airfields at Foggia. They wanted to put 6,000 men of the British 1st Airborne Division into the heel of Italy and send them up the east coast toward Foggia. But the Salerno landings were using all the available transports. So, while Clark's army landed, the British navy took a daring gamble. Admiral Sir Andrew Browne Cunningham, Eisenhower's naval chief, sent the 1st Airborne men aboard a small battle fleet—the battleship *Howe* and four cruisers—to the port of Taranto. This force had to sail right past a large division of the Italian fleet, and no one was certain that the Italian navy was obeying Badoglio's instructions to surrender. It was. There was no engagement. One British cruiser hit a floating mine and sank, losing 200 men. The rest of the troops were delivered safely to the Taranto docks, where they disembarked like passengers leaving a cruise ship. Immediately they started north toward Foggia.

The crucial battle for Salerno Bay began when Kesselring counterattacked with his tanks in full strength. By D-Plus-Three, the Germans had reinforced the 16th Panzer with parts of five other tank divisions. They struck fast and hard from Eboli against the center of Clark's enlarged, unified beachhead. Moving down the north bank of the Sele River, they split that part of Clark's front into isolated, confused small groups. The fighting was furious. Some key positions—a tobacco factory and a bridge among them —changed hands repeatedly.

One German armored column forced a 45th Division regiment out of the town of Persano, and then rolled forward to overrun a 36th Division battalion.

When the Germans were finally stopped, they were no more than two miles from the shore. Kesselring, hearing the early reports of his army's successes, was confident that he was about to drive through the Fifth Army and divide it in two. For some time, it looked as if he might.

The Americans and the British hung on, using their field artillery well. Eisenhower ordered his air chief, Marshal Sir Arthur Tedder, to send up every plane that could fly to Salerno. The great air strike, beginning on the night of the 13th and continuing through the morning of September 14th, seemed to rock all southern Italy to its foundations. Naval fire support added thousands of shells to the crescendo of Allied bombing and firing. German field headquarters at Eboli was set on fire. To one 45th Division infantryman who was watching, the flames seemed to light the entire night sky.

By D-Plus-6 (September 15th) Clark's troops knew the crisis was past. A last German tank thrust lacked the power of earlier efforts. And reinforcements were reaching the Allied lines. Kesselring had missed his chance—if only by a little. On the 16th he ordered a German withdrawal to the north. He was fighting for time to destroy Naples.

Montgomery's 5th Division made contact with the Salerno forces, completing a splendid advance of 250 miles up the Italian west coast in two weeks. On the east coast the 1st Airborne, fighting like infantry, was at Bari, considerably short of Foggia. Not enemy action but Allied supply problems—especially lack of gasoline—held them up.

The Germans could delay the advance of the Fifth Army but they couldn't stop it. Clark's men fought past the ruins of Pompeii, around Mount Vesuvius, and entered Naples on October 1st. Besides wrecking the port, the retreating Germans had tried to knock out the entire city. They smashed the water and electrical supply systems, wiped out the flour mills, razed the principal hotels, and planted booby traps everywhere. They had gone to considerable trouble to destroy the University of Naples (founded in 1224) with hand grenades and gasoline. Allied bombs had also done tremendous damage to Naples, but the German destruction seemed spiteful because it went far beyond military needs. The Nazis destroyed much that was of use only to Italian civilians.

The port of Naples, choked with more than fifty wrecked ships, was a mess. Allied engineers and sea salvage experts immediately started work. Many Neapolitans helped. Four Italian submarines supplied electricity for the work. In less than a month, the "impossible" had been accomplished: Naples was again a working port, handling 5,000 tons of supplies a day for the Allied front.

Montgomery's Eighth Army captured the Foggia

airfields just before the Fifth Army entered Naples. The British force continued to push ahead, up the east coast as far as Termoli.

The first phase of the Italian campaign was won.

Things had gone so well on the whole that Eisenhower and Alexander thought for a time that the British and American forces could quickly drive on to Rome. Kesselring, whose defensive front now stretched across Italy from west to east, was ready to dispute the point. The German commander persuaded Hitler that the Allies could be held for some time with a defense-in-depth starting at the Volturno River, not far north of Naples. Autumn rains were starting, and the battle-grounds were turning to mud, a factor that favored the defenders. Germany still held two-thirds of Italy, including the industrial north. Kesselring saw no sense in withdrawing any farther.

Northern Italy was a German puppet state. Mussolini had been rescued by the Germans in a spectacular glider raid on a small hotel at Gran Sasso, in the Abruzzi mountains. There the deposed dictator had been hidden by the Badoglio government. Mussolini was tired, old, and physically worn almost beyond recognition. He didn't even want to pretend to play the game, but he proclaimed the "restoration" of the Fascist regime, and was obeyed only where the German army was in power. Surrounded by a bodyguard of German soldiers, who were really his jailors, Mussolini was a walking ghost who did whatever Hitler demanded.

Months of desperately hard fighting lay ahead in Italy, but after October, 1943, the forthcoming cross-Channel assault from England to France outranked all other Allied efforts in the European war. The invasion, called OVERLORD, was still eight or nine months away, and as yet the plans were scarcely more than an outline with tens of thousands of details to be filled in. But OVERLORD called for a buildup in England of men and materials on a scale larger than any previous amphibious attack in military history. These ambitious plans were possible because the British and American navies had won the Battle of the Atlantic.

Hitler's great hopes for his U-boat offensive had lasted long after the Casablanca Conference. In March, 1943, for instance, the Germans had sunk 108 Allied vessels. But something like a turning point had been reached in early May. Forty-two merchant ships were being convoyed west across the Atlantic by a British escort group of nine ships and two Catalina seaplanes —one American and the other Canadian—commanded by Commander P. W. Gretton of the British Royal Navy. A wolfpack of fifty-one U-boats attacked. Gretton's small fleet struck right back. The running fight continued for ten days, in impossibly foul weather.

The Germans sent thirteen Allied freighters to the bottom, but they lost seven U-boats in the effort. It was too high a price for the Germans. From that battle on, the situation improved for the Allies.

Bombers based in southern England, coöperating with fast-moving corvettes, spoiled Doenitz' favorite submarine base, the French Bay of Biscay. And new microwave radar was able to spot surfaced U-boats in the dark. If the bombers couldn't sink the enemy submarines, the corvettes often could.

The Allies lost forty-one ships in May, but the Germans lost thirty-eight submarines.

In June, Doenitz' raiders sent down only six Allied ships, at a cost so high that he withdrew, for the time being, from the transatlantic sea lanes.

That same month, the United States destroyer-escort building program got into full swing after having been delayed because of the greater need for beaching and landing craft. By the end of the year, more than 200 new destroyer escorts had been commissioned. United States production of Liberator bombers was also rising fast, and the 900-mile range of the new planes made them good for anti-submarine duty. Mid-ocean was still dangerous, but it no longer held its earlier terrors. Then, late in 1943, Portugal gave the Allies permission to base anti-submarine planes in the Azores—and Doenitz' Black Pit was eliminated forever.

Hitler now counted on secret super-weapons, instead of submarine warfare, to win the war for him. German scientists were indeed doing some amazing work. At Peenemunde, a secret island experimental station in the Baltic Sea, a flying bomb (V-1) and the world's first supersonic guided missile (V-2) were in their final stages of development. They were both capable of doing tremendous damage. There was no defense at all against the V-2.

Knowing that something unusual was going on at Peenemunde, the R.A.F. attacked it on August 17th, with a great armada of 597 Lancaster and Halifax bombers. They blew the experimental station to bits before the German fighters could retaliate. The brilliant moon, which had helped the bombers' attack, also helped the defense. The R.A.F. lost 40 planes with 240 crew members. But the damage delayed German rocketry production more than a month, a delay the Germans could not afford.

The great Allied air offensive was growing. British and American strategic bombers were flying more than 5,000 missions and dropping more than 10,000 tons of bombs a month. Their deadly pounding of the German war machine was on the point of tenfold increase. Some German cities had almost been obliterated. Hamburg was one example. A series of four raids, using incendiary bombs for the most part, had destroyed an average of every other building in that port, including 4,000 factories. Antwerp, Cologne, Duisberg, Essen, Kiel, and Kassel had been heavily damaged.

Since oil and gasoline are as essential to modern war as steel and gunpowder, the oilfields and refineries at Ploesti, Rumania, were another target for the Allies. According to Allied intelligence, that cluster of installations was supplying one-quarter of the Axis' natural (as contrasted with synthetic) petroleum products. The Allied victory in North Africa had provided a base—Bengasi, Libya—from which they could try a daring, low-level raid on Ploesti.

On the first of August, 177 U.S. B-24 Liberators took off across the Mediterranean. But unexpectedly heavy clouds obscured the target, and two groups of bombers made wrong turns. Worse, the squadrons had been spotted on their way. When the slightly disorganized Liberator formations came into Ploesti at treetop level, enemy flak and fighter planes were waiting. The raid did considerable damage, but it didn't wipe out Ploesti, as the Allies had hoped. American losses were painfully high.

Seventeen days later, from bases in England, 376 Flying Fortresses attacked Regensburg and Schweinfurt, near Munich. The bombers were out to destroy the German ball-bearing industry. The raid did much damage, but it was as difficult a mission as any the Eighth Air Force ever had to fly. For one thing, the targets were far beyond the range of Allied fighter escorts, and German fighter units attacked all the way. The Forts showed their tremendous fire power and shot down 288 enemy planes. But sixty Allied bombers were lost. It was once again evident that the new P-51 Mustang fighter planes, with their greater range, could not arrive a minute too soon. It was just as clear that, as Allied air power mounted, Hitler was going to have trouble keeping British and American planes from ruling the skies over western Europe.

Meanwhile, the German armies were losing all along the gigantic Eastern front. For the third successive summer, Hitler had mounted a strong offensive against the Russians. He had thrown half a million men—including seventeen panzer divisions equipped with new tanks—against the Red Army near Kursk and Orel, 200 miles south of Moscow. The Germans made some progress. Then the Russians counterattacked, at the same time the British and Americans were invading Sicily. Hitler stopped the Kursk offensive, explaining that several panzer divisions had to be transferred immediately to the West.

Stalin's forces had gained strength during the year. The Russian artillery, air force, and armored units had been increased. There were roughly four Russian soldiers to every German, and the Russians were better trained than they had been in 1942. The Russian counterattack gradually spread along the whole front, from Kirov to Novorossisk on the Black Sea. In August the Red Army retook Orel and Kharkov; in September, Poltava and Smolensk. The sheer weight of Russian attacks forced the Germans back, no matter how skillfully they fought. Hitler's order, repeated again and again— to stand and fight for every inch of ground—merely increased the German losses.

The progress the Allies made in 1943 was almost greater than they had dared hope.

9
CASSINO AND ANZIO

Clark's Fifth Army and Montgomery's Eighth Army continued north from Naples and Termoli, with Americans on the left and the British on the right. Their combined strength was only eleven divisions. The rough mountainous terrain confined the Allied attacks to the obvious routes up valleys, with little chance for maneuver or surprise. The bitter, muddy succession of frontal attacks was an infantryman's nightmare. Wherever the Germans yielded they blew up the bridges, demolished the roads cut out of the rocky mountainsides, and then emplaced well-hidden machine guns and mortars to cover the obstacles. Nonetheless, Fifth Army engineers repaired the damage, using Sherman tanks converted into bulldozers. The "tank-dozers" protected the men from everything except heavy artillery and large mines.

The British and American divisions forced their way across the Volturno and Biferno rivers, the southern boundaries of Kesselring's defense-in-depth. By the middle of November, Clark and Montgomery had reached the enemy's main line of resistance, thirty miles farther north. The German Winter Line ran from the Garigliano River on the west, past Mount Majo and Cassino, to the Sangro River on the east. There the slow Allied advance bogged down, seventy-five miles short of Rome. But though the Allies were not gaining ground as they had hoped, the eleven British and American divisions were occupying almost twice that many German soldiers—troops that might otherwise have been moved to the Russian front, or to France to get ready to repel a cross-Channel assault.

Constant meetings had taken place in 1943 between the British and American strategists: at Washington, D.C. (May), Quebec (August), Cairo (November and December), and—with the Russians included—Teheran (November). All of the conferences had been difficult. It sometimes had seemed impossible for any two, let alone three, of the Allies to agree on a single point, and each meeting raised hundreds of questions of priority, schedule, and command. Above all loomed the problem of the actual shape of the Allied effort.

One of Hitler's sustaining hopes—besides the secret weapons he was developing—was that the United States, Great Britain, and the Soviet Union would break up their alliance because of their disagreements. The disagreements were indeed fierce. But there was never a moment when the complicated arguments among the Allies approached an explosion point. Their shared hatred of Hitler and his tyrannical regime kept them together.

The conference at Teheran ended all debates about the supreme importance of OVERLORD and a supporting invasion through southern France, called ANVIL. Stalin agreed with Roosevelt that these were more promising than any new actions in the Mediterranean—opening the Dardanelles, for instance, or bringing Turkey into the war on the Allied side, or stirring up trouble for Hitler in the Balkans, or establishing a small beachhead on the Dalmatian or Albanian coasts. (Churchill and his advisers had thought that these might be worth trying.)

On his way home from the second Cairo conference in December of 1943, President Roosevelt flew to Tunis. Without explaining why, he had asked Eisenhower, who was busy directing operations in Italy, to meet him there. The President's plane touched down in midafternoon, and he was helped into a waiting automobile. Eisenhower got in beside him. Almost immediately Roosevelt broke the most exciting news that the General, up to that point, had ever heard: "Well, Ike, you had better start packing. You are going to command OVERLORD."

Eisenhower was especially surprised because he had expected this assignment to go to General George C. Marshall, chairman of the Joint Chiefs of Staff. Roosevelt, however, had finally decided he wanted Marshall, one of his most trusted advisers, near him in Washington.

In a talk over the radio on Christmas Eve, President Roosevelt announced to the world Eisenhower's new title: "Supreme Commander, Allied Expeditionary Force." The phrase worried Commander Harry Butcher, Eisenhower's naval aide. He did not see how he could design stationery dignified enough to carry the imposing title.

By Christmas Day, Eisenhower had told General Bradley that he was going to command all the United States ground forces in the Normandy invasion. Montgomery had the matching assignment on the British side.

The bitter fighting in Italy continued. By January, 1944, after three unsuccessful attempts to break Kesselring's Winter Line, Clark's Fifth Army was battering its way forward near the junction of the valleys of two rivers, the Liri and the Rapido. Monte Cassino, a 1,400-year-old monastery, stood on top of a dominating hill. A huge building with yellow stone walls, it was a repository of European culture. Cassino, the monastery and the ancient, thick-walled town below, was the keystone of the Germans' defense.

On January 17, 1944, the Fifth Army tried a new attack. The U.S. 34th and 36th Infantry divisions moved straight ahead toward Cassino. On their left, the British Tenth Corps pushed across the lower Garigliano River, trying to draw off German strength to the west. On the right, two French divisions which had just come into the Allied line, the 3rd Algerian and the 2nd Moroccan, advanced through the mountains toward the peaks north of Cassino.

The British and French flank attacks went fairly well. But the Americans in the center had a brutal time trying to cross the Rapido River in their assault boats. Only one battalion of the 36th Division got to the far side. The men established a shallow beachhead some 500 yards long, but their toe hold couldn't be reinforced. From the high ground around Monte Cassino, the Germans saw every move the Americans made, and they poured mortar and shellfire into the improvised position. The enemy's *nebelwerfer,* a six-barreled mortar, seemed sixty times more devastating than the ordinary single-barreled mortar. The battalion clung to the far bank for two nights. When it withdrew, its total casualties were more than 1,000— practically its entire strength.

While the main offensive was coming to a halt on the Rapido, an amphibious British-American corps, commanded by American Major General John P. Lucas, was moving north from Naples by sea. It was headed for Anzio and Nettuno, two small towns on the west coast of Italy which were sixty miles behind the German lines and more than two-thirds of the way to Rome.

Lucas' force, VI Corps, was almost as large as the army that had landed at Salerno: 50,000 men, 5,000 vehicles. In spite of its great size—200 ships—the corps' fleet sailed 120 miles without being spotted by the enemy. At 2:00 A.M. on the morning of January 22, 1944, the U.S. 3rd Infantry Division began going ashore a little south of Nettuno. It met next to no opposition, and quickly captured the valuable bridges across the Mussolini Canal. By midmorning the division commander, Major General Lucian Truscott, radioed that he had secured his D-Day objectives and was ready for further orders.

The British 1st Division went ashore just north of Anzio, and by noon had pushed two miles inland. British commandos blocked the Albano Road to seal off the beachhead, and American Rangers easily captured Anzio itself. The port was intact. It went into operation almost immediately, handling incoming troops and supplies.

The Allies had achieved perfect surprise. The towns

were guarded by only two German battalions, which had been sent there to rest. Kesselring had mistaken the British feint across the Garigliano for a major Allied offensive, and, just before the Anzio-Nettuno landings, had committed all his mobile troops to meet that imaginary threat.

No one on the Allied side guessed how badly off balance the Germans were. Ten miles inland from the Anzio beachhead lay the Alban Hills. Just beyond them, ran the main route from Rome to the German front lines in the south. Kesselring correctly supposed that this road was an Allied objective. While Lucas methodically set about expanding his beachhead and preparing to move forward in strength, Kesselring scratched around for troops to defend at Anzio. He found some in Rome. He called for part of a division from Genoa, another from Rimini. He took the 1st Parachute Corps away from the Rapido River front.

During the next week, every time VI Corps patrols took a German prisoner, he belonged to a different outfit. Allied Intelligence officers imagined that each new unit they identified was there at full strength. Remembering Kesselring's counterattack at Salerno and fearing, in view of the stalemate along the Winter Line, to take chances, VI Corps became security-minded. Mines were planted, wire was strung, and every precaution was taken against a German counter-attack.

By the night of January 29th, when Lucas finally attacked, Kesselring's desperate patchwork of bits and pieces of divisions formed a fairly solid defensive line around the Allied beachhead. The two Ranger battalions that led the assault ran into overwhelming opposition and the Allied attack was thrown back with the loss of 800 men. The Rangers had run right into a German counterattack force, formed up and ready to go.

Though the Rangers were defeated, they had disorganized the Germans. It took Kesselring almost three weeks to prepare another assault. By the time it started, on February 16th, the German commander had pulled together a very strong force. He hurled most of nine German divisions against the Anzio position, and his armor made one deep cut into the VI Corps beachhead, down the Albano-Anzio road.

But Lucas' cautious buildup of strength within the beachhead now paid off. The defenses were too strong for the attackers. The corps' 800 guns plastered the danger point with shellfire, and the Allied lines held. Kesselring pulled back, content for the moment to fortify his lines around the beachhead.

10

THE CAPTURE OF ROME

For the next three months, while the great preparations for OVERLORD went ahead in England, there was practically no change at Anzio. Truscott took over the VI Corps from Lucas, and the men of his seven divisions (two British, five American) held their eighty square miles of ground. They dug in deeper and deeper, piling their sandbags higher and higher to protect themselves from incessant German artillery fire and from the bombs the Luftwaffe dropped into the beachhead night after night.

German shellfire could reach every part of the British-American position, and German observation from the Alban Hills was excellent. Good observation, however, was scarcely needed. VI Corps' troops were so crowded that any stray 88-millimeter shell was likely to hit something. Although Truscott's artillery kept firing back, and the Allied air forces practically controlled the sky during the day, life at Anzio was an ordeal. Allied casualty lists grew at a nerve-wracking rate—ten percent of the troops being killed and wounded in action each month.

No Allied offensive was planned for the time being, but the infantry companies in the front lines had to be on constant alert. Every night, patrols were sent out to harass the Germans and find out what they were doing.

Although night patrolling is army routine, to the men doing the job it is a terrifying life-and-death ordeal. One March night, for instance, Lieutenant William C. Landgren of the 179th Regiment, 45th Infantry Division, led a routine patrol into the darkness just ahead of his company's right front. He took another officer, Lieutenant Willard Peters, and sixteen men with him.

Landgren's mission was to advance just a few hundred yards to a wrecked ambulance at the side of the road. During the day some Germans had been spotted near the wreck. The question was whether they were engaged in anything important.

A compass reading was all the patrol had to keep them headed in the right direction. The men moved in single file, slowly, and as quietly as possible. Friendly artillery shells fluttered over their heads and landed with a C-r-u-m-p deep in the Germans' positions. German shells, headed the other way, cracked past. Either sound was enough to make a man's heart skip a beat, but the patrol's overriding fear was that of being detected by German infantrymen.

After the patrol had gone 100 yards, Landgren dropped off Peters and five men as a listening post. The others spread out into a V, with Landgren, a runner, and a squad sergeant at the point. They moved on, half walking, half crawling, taking advantage of shell holes for cover.

Suddenly a German flare lit the scene. Evidently some enemy outpost had heard the patrol coming. As soon as the flare burned out, Landgren moved forward again.

Then Landgren heard a noise directly ahead. He and the two others next to him froze in their tracks, peering ahead into the darkness. A German patrol was coming right at them!

Landgren opened fire. The Germans fired back. The exchange showed Landgren that his advance party was outnumbered. He sent his runner back to bring up Peters' men. Rifle shots cracked back and forth. The Germans tossed two or three concussion grenades at the Americans. Then they withdrew.

Landgren checked over his squad. To his relief, no one had been hit. But the night's work wasn't done.

116

The patrol was still some distance from the wrecked ambulance. Landgren listened carefully. Hearing nothing, he ordered the patrol to form up again. It went ahead.

Near the ambulance, Landgren found a German soldier in a shell hole. The German was eager to surrender. Landgren's patrol got back safely—perhaps only because of the assistance of their prisoner. He told them that the Americans had just walked through a German mine field. They had escaped injury purely by luck. The German guided Landgren's men through the mines on the return trip.

In the after-action report of that night, Landgren's patrol was scarcely worth mentioning. It was only one of dozens along the VI Corps front. Nothing unusual had happened.

While the men at Anzio held on, the 34th Infantry Division took up the Cassino-Monte Cassino attack where the 36th had failed. The 34th crossed the Rapido River farther upstream. The Germans had blown a dam, flooding the river valley and turning it into a bog. The division waded through the mud to the far side, and established a bridgehead it could hold. But when it tried to turn left and batter its way down the far bank of the Rapido to the town of Cassino, it ran into a wall of German resistance. Despite the reinforcements they had sent to Anzio, the Germans on the Winter Line were somewhat stronger than before.

It was clear that they could hold out in the town of Cassino. The monastery's hill would have to be taken.

The 34th struggled into the mountains, crawling from one hill to the next, in an effort to capture Monte Cassino from behind. The weather was bitterly cold. There was no way an infantryman could dig a foxhole; the best he could do was scrape together a little nest of rocks around himself. The Germans, who had blasted out mortar and artillery positions when they first set up their defenses, resisted every foot of the way. Still the 34th kept going. Some of its battalions were down to twenty percent of strength. By February 11th, the 34th had entirely exhausted itself in battle. When it got the order to withdraw, fifty infantrymen still in the line, still firing, were so weak and numb from the cold that they had to be carried down the mountain on litters. For the time being, the 34th could fight no farther, but it had gained priceless ground. In one place the Allied line had been pushed as close as 1,000 yards to the monastery's ridge.

Two fresh Allied divisions, the 2nd New Zealand and the 4th Indian, took over where the 34th left off. Fifth Army had refrained from bombing the abbey itself, but on February 15th, Monte Cassino was blasted by 112 medium and 142 bombers of the Strategic Air Command. Then the New Zealanders attacked the hill with great bravery and spirit. They got next to nowhere.

As spring approached, the south of England began to resemble a vast parking lot. Tens of thousands of trucks, half-tracks, tanks, command cars, and jeeps were scattered over the landscape under draped camouflage nets. Ammunition dumps were everywhere. If you could find a square foot of open field that did not contain military materiel of some kind, there was likely to be a soldier on it. There were to be only six divisions (three American, two British, and one Canadian) in the D-Day landings, but the planners in Eisenhower's headquarters were looking ahead, far beyond the landings, to the battles inland. The Allied Expeditionary Force was going to include a total of 2,800,000 men. If all went well, Eisenhower hoped that 725,000 men and 95,000 vehicles, with all the supplies they needed, would be put ashore in Normandy during OVERLORD's first two weeks.

The men in the three American assault divisions—the 1st, the 4th, and the 29th—had known for several months that their units were among those who would lead the way. Any worry they might originally have felt had given way to the feeling that the sooner D-Day came the better. Their training had been exceedingly hard, with a heavy emphasis on physical fitness. Considering all that the 1st Division had been through in North Africa and Sicily, a training program was almost insulting. But the 1st had had so many replacements, including a new commanding officer, Major

General Clarence R. Huebner, that it was partly a new outfit.

The same was true of Ridgway's 82nd Airborne Division. With the 101st Airborne, commanded by General Maxwell Taylor, Ridgway's division had been chosen to drop into the Cotentin Peninsula—the extreme right of the Allied front—five hours before the seaborne troops came ashore. The invasion would need a good port, and Cherbourg, at the tip of the Cotentin, would be able to handle the reinforcements and supplies. The American paratroopers, with the 4th Division, were expected to stop the Germans from reinforcing their defenses at Cherbourg.

All the details of OVERLORD were top secret. Twenty-two hundred CIC (Counter-Intelligence Corps) agents in England were trying to keep them a secret. But the buildup could easily be seen by German reconnaissance planes, not to mention German spies. Furthermore, the American assault divisions had a full dress rehearsal for D-Day at the end of April. They put to sea in landing craft and attacked the beaches at Slapton Sands, near Dartmouth on England's southern coast. Not only were Germans watching, but a German torpedo-boat slipped through the Allies' protective screen of naval vessels and sank two LSTs. Seven hundred men were lost.

Though the enemy knew an assault would come, it didn't know the date or place. Eisenhower was doing his best to fool Rommel and Field Marshal Karl von Rundstedt, who now commanded the opposing forces, into thinking that the main Allied effort would land at the Pas de Calais. That is the part of the French coast nearest to England, north of Normandy. The Allies also tried to make the enemy think that D-Day was scheduled for the middle of July, not the first week in June. In spite of a very few security slip-ups, the secrets of time and place were kept.

But Hitler was taking no chances. He had directed a vast effort, costing millions of man hours, to fortify the entire western coast of Europe from Denmark to Spain. His "Atlantic Wall," as the Fuehrer called it, was 860 miles long. It was not a wall at all, but something stronger: underwater obstacles laced with mines to blow the bottoms out of beaching craft, mined beaches, barbed wire, coastal guns in concrete emplacements, concrete bunkers, pillboxes, forts, machine-gun nests, and trench systems. Farther inland, wherever a glider might land, posts were planted, wired together, and equipped with Teller mines. After his return from Africa, Rommel had put the finishing touches on Hitler's Atlantic Wall. He thought it would slow down any invasion force long enough for the Germans to counterattack and drive the invaders into the sea.

Right after the Slapton Sands rehearsal, the assault and follow-up divisions went into camps near the ports where they would embark. On army maps, each camp was an irregular circle; thus they earned the name "sausages." Detailed briefings began while the troops checked over their equipment, smeared all their engines with a greasy compound, and attached breather pipes so their vehicles could be driven through deep water for a few minutes without stalling. All training stopped. All the usual army "housekeeping" chores for the 55,000 assault troops were taken care of by other soldiers. Even the assault cooks were relieved from cooking and were waited on instead. An armored division that was scheduled to land long after D-Day did most of the dirty work, to its members' deep disgust.

The assault troops found it hard to get used to this sudden coddling.

"I'd like it better," remarked a private in one of the assault divisions, "if they would treat me a little meaner."

Both the Allied strategic bombing and tactical air forces were over France day and night. The air offensive mounted close to 45,000 sorties each month. In all France, the Germans had fifty-eight divisions. About seventeen of them were stationed in the northwestern corner of the country, where the invasion would land. The Allied air attacks were designed to cut off Normandy and Brittany—an area about the size of the State of Indiana—making it impossible for the remaining forty-one divisions to rush to the aid of the seventeen. Troop movement within that area was to be made as difficult as possible for the Germans. The Allied air forces attacked all forms of enemy transport—their main targets being bridges and railways.

In addition, the Allied airmen were trying to beat the Luftwaffe, plane by plane, in the sky. Eisenhower wanted absolute control of the air over the English Channel. In the month of May alone, 1,000 German planes were shot down and 900 locomotives and 16,000 freight cars were hit. Meanwhile, the Allied navies were making sure that no German submarines were in position to attack the invasion fleet. They were also clearing the Channel of floating mines.

The assault troops, completely sealed off from the rest of England and the world, were largely unaware of all that was being done on their behalf—except for the vast formations of planes they saw going and coming. For the time being, they took it easy.

During the second week of May, the Allied front in Italy exploded into action. General Alexander put all the Allied weight on the extreme left of his line, the twenty-mile stretch between Cassino and the sea. Clark's Fifth Army and the British Eighth Army, now commanded by Lieutenant General Sir Oliver Leese, had been greatly strengthened. The long stalemate was

123

broken. Both Allied armies forged ahead past Cassino and Monte Cassino. The Germans had to pull back. Cassino was finally taken, on May 18th, by the Eighth Army's Polish Corps. This unit was made up of exiles who had either managed to escape from their ravaged country or from German and Russian prisoner-of-war camps.

On May 23rd, Truscott's VI Corps smashed its way out of the Anzio beachhead through Cisterna, where the Rangers had lost so heavily, and made good progress toward Valmontone, east of the Alban Hills. Two days later the Fifth Army, advancing up the Italian coast, made contact with VI Corps. Anzio was a beachhead no longer, but part of the Fifth Army's front.

For a while it looked as if Truscott might push on to Valmontone, cut the main highway down the Sacco River Valley, and trap an entire German army of ten divisions between the British and the Americans. Unfortunately Clark, in his eagerness to get to Rome, had Truscott send only the 3rd Infantry Division with an armored task force toward Valmontone. He switched VI Corps' main effort—made by the 34th, the 45th, the 36th and the 1st Armored—to the northwest toward the Alban Hills, on both sides of the Naples-Rome railroad. Clark's change of direction gave the German I Parachute Corps, composed of three fine divisions, a chance to dig in. They fought furiously. Tired after three days of heavy fighting, the 3rd Division could not quite cut the highway. The Germans escaped from the trap.

Still, the delay was only temporary. On June 4th, with the 36th Division leading the way, the Americans arrived in Rome. The Germans had left the great city only hours earlier. The lead tank in Clark's column had two Italians, serving as guides, riding on its hatch. The Fifth Army's triumph was completed without a single shot.

THE WAR IN FRANCE AND GERMANY

American D-Day assault troops land at Omaha Beach on the northern coast of France.
(U.S. Army)

On Utah Beach, troops take a "breather" behind a concrete wall, preparing to follow their "buddies" over the crest.
(U.S. Army)

U.S. infantrymen advance under machine-gun fire into the outskirts of Brest. *(UPI)*

Antiaircraft batteries protect the vital Remagen bridge captured intact by the Allies. *(Wide World)*

Under heavy enemy fire, soldiers of the U.S. First Army crouch for the attack on a heavily fortified area of the Siegfried Line. *(Wide World)*

American gunners roll a 57-mm. gun down a German street. *(Wide World)*

11
CROSS-CHANNEL ATTACK

Meanwhile, OVERLORD was proceeding on schedule. By Saturday, June 3rd, the Normandy invasion troops were loaded in the transports, ready to go. D-Day was set for June 4th. Then the weather forecast, which had already been discouraging, turned bad.

It was not especially hard for Eisenhower to order a 24-hour delay, even though part of the invasion fleet —ships already crossing the Irish Sea because they had the farthest to sail—had to be sent back to port. But if the attack could not proceed on the 6th or the 7th, it would have to be postponed for two weeks or a month waiting for a suitable combination of moon and tides. The location of the five beaches (their army code names were Sword, Juno, Gold, Omaha, and

Utah) could hardly be kept secret even two weeks longer—not when 140,000 men knew where they were. And during any long wait, the spirits of the keyed-up assault troops would sag.

Yet Eisenhower and his staff knew that practically everything, from the actual beaching to the all-important last-minute bombing of the German defenses, depended on good weather.

On June 4th, the SHAEF weather experts predicted at least a 36-hour interval between two storms. The better weather would last through the 6th and 7th. Eisenhower weighed the risks of waiting against the risks of going. At 4:15 on the morning of June 5th, he decided there was nothing to do but go the following day.

D-Day was to be June 6th, 1944. Orders were immediately transmitted down through the complicated chain of Allied command, and the great fleet of 6,000 ships began to move. Win or lose, there was no longer a chance of stopping the effort.

Eisenhower had faced almost the same problem with the weather on the eve of the invasion of Sicily. Here again, his luck was good. Before many hours passed, the storm started to slacken.

By midnight on the 5th, most of the troop transports lay quietly at anchor, 10,000 yards or more off the Normandy shore. The crossing had been merely a little choppy. But the Germans had been fooled by

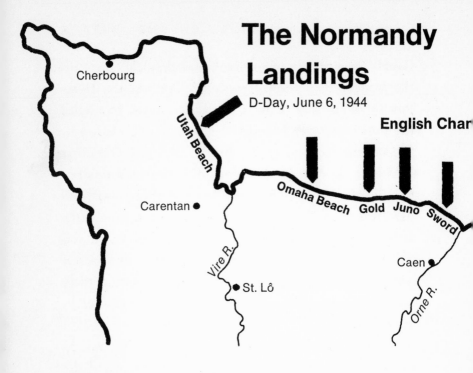

The Normandy Landings

D-Day, June 6, 1944

Cherbourg

Utah Beach

English Char

Carentan

Omaha Beach Gold Juno Sword

Vire R.

St. Lô

Caen

Orne R.

the weather into thinking the invasion was temporarily impossible. With no weather stations in Greenland or the North Atlantic, they had been unable to forecast the break between storms.

At 1:30 A.M. on the 6th, exactly five hours before the first waves of infantrymen were to hit the beaches, the parachute drops began. Although there was a full moon, the night sky was hazy with patches of thick, low clouds. The British 6th Airborne, using parachutes and gliders, did well on the east end of the 50-mile invasion coast. They took the bridges they were trying to save (across the Orne River and the Caen

Canal) in a matter of minutes, and they also blew up the bridges they wanted to destroy (across the Dives River). They moved back toward the coast to silence the gun battery at Merville before it had a chance to fire on the oncoming 3rd British and 3rd Canadian Divisions. To the west, behind Utah Beach, Ridgway's 82nd Airborne and Taylor's 101st Airborne—12,000 parachutists, and 4,000 men in gliders—ran into heavy antiaircraft fire. The low-lying clouds concealed the American navigators' checkpoints. The two drops were badly scattered and many gliders, missing their landing points, cracked up and split open like matchboxes.

But the paratroopers of both divisions were trained to expect the unexpected. Despite confusion and demoralizing casualties, they began to form improvised squads, platoons, and company-sized units. Taylor's men soon captured the narrow causeways leading inland from the beach. Ridgway's outfit was working its way toward the town of Ste. Mère Église to establish a firm base, shield the 4th Division's beach, and stop any enemy attempt to reinforce Cherbourg. As in Sicily, the crazy pattern of the drops bewildered the local German commanders. They did not know what to defend because they couldn't figure out what was being attacked.

German Seventh Army Headquarters flashed word to von Rundstedt, in his villa outside Paris, that paratroopers were landing. (Rommel was in Germany, conferring with Hitler.) Von Rundstedt was too experienced to be hurried. He was also a little bit too sure that the main Allied invasion would come in the Pas de Calais area. He thought the paratroopers were a preliminary diversion. To be on the safe side, von Rundstedt ordered two German divisions to move toward Caen. But, luckily for the Allies, the German chain of command was not clear cut, and Hitler had postponed untangling the confusion. His highest army command headquarters *(Oberkommando der Wehrmacht)* delayed the execution of von Rundstedt's order.

At 3:15 A.M., the vast preparatory bombardment by 1,100 R.A.F. heavy bombers began with a sweep of the whole French coast, from the mouth of the Seine to Cherbourg. At 5:50 A.M., the 700 warships in the invasion fleet began to fire on their targets all along the beaches. The eight-inch shells of the battleships, like the *Texas*, the *Augusta*, the *Arkansas*, the *Warspite*, and the *Ramillies*, rumbled over the heads of the assault troops.

Combat engineers were moving in toward the beaches with equipment to clear lanes through the mines and underwater obstacles. The amphibious Sherman tanks (DDs—standing for Dual Drive) had been launched. They were scheduled to move through the cleared lanes, right ahead of the first infantry waves. But soon they were in trouble. The moderate sea was too rough for them; there was a nasty slap to the waves. Some of the tanks had shipped so much water on starting that they were already beginning to sink.

At 6:00 A.M., 1,365 heavy bombers of the U.S. Eighth Air Force pounded the invasion coast. At 6:15 the medium and fighter bombers of the Ninth Air Force came in low. They aimed at the most menacing gun positions in the German beach fortifications. The noise of the exploding bombs and shells made it sound as if there would be little of Normandy left for the infantrymen to take.

But this did not turn out to be the case. Because of the morning haze, the bombers' target lines had been pushed inland to keep them from hitting Allied troops by mistake. The men in the first waves were about to discover that many of the beach fortifications had scarcely been damaged at all. A vast number of Germans, and German guns, had survived the tremendous preparatory bombardment.

At 6:30, H-Hour, the first of the small assault boats lowered their ramps and spilled their teams of wet, cold soldiers onto Sword, Juno, Gold, Omaha and Utah beaches. The Germans began shooting at them as soon as they were visible.

On both flanks, the assault went slowly but well. The British divisions and the 3rd Canadian moved in fairly easily. The U.S. 4th Division landing, thanks to the good work of the paratroopers behind Utah Beach, met far less enemy fire than it had expected.

But in the center, at Omaha Beach, the going was unexpectedly tough. There the 1st Division, on the left, and the 29th Division, on the right, were making the main Allied effort. Twenty-seven DD tanks had failed to make it to Omaha, and the air bombardment had missed almost all of the beach's key defenses. The engineer battalions had cleared only a few lanes. And because of rough water the LCVPs and other beaching craft carried the soldiers to the wrong landing places. The strong west-to-east current swept the small assault boats from 200 to as many as 1,000 yards to the left. The well-spaced plan was jumbled. The high ground behind Omaha Beach was hidden in smoky haze. Many of the men in the first assault wave did not know where they were, or where they were supposed to go. Nothing that they saw around them looked like the maps they had studied. Yet the troops waiting to follow expected them to demolish what was left on Omaha of Hitler's Atlantic Wall.

To make matters still worse, one first-rate German division, the 352nd Infantry, was in the Omaha Beach area for anti-invasion maneuvers. Allied intelligence thought it had left. But it hadn't. The German division was ready, alert, and standing squarely in the path of Major General Leonard T. Gerow's V Corps.

The first and second assault waves got practically nowhere. The attack went in by boat sections, each made up of thirty-two men. In some sections all the men were killed or wounded before they got out of the water. Since the tide was rising fast, many of the wounded were drowned. No one reached the high grassy bluffs behind the beach. The Germans still held the five draws—the rising, narrow roads that were to serve as the main exits from Omaha. At the end of the first hour—7:30 A.M.—the attack had not advanced as far as it should have in the first five minutes.

Most of the surviving men had managed to cross the sandy flats through German shell and small-arms fire to a low sea wall, two-thirds of the distance to the bluffs. Many of them were in a state of near shock from the cold, seasickness, and the effectiveness of the enemy's shooting. The attack was disorganized, seemingly beyond repair. Nevertheless twenty or thirty men, scattered at random along Omaha's 7,000 yards, had approximately the same thought at about the same time: This is so bad, I might as well try to do something.

And they did something. A private named Ingram E. Lambert (C Company, 116th Regiment) climbed over the sea wall with a long bangalore torpedo in his arms and planted the explosive charge under the barbed wire on the far side. Lambert was killed immediately, but his platoon leader, 2nd Lieutenant

Stanley M. Schwartz, followed, exploded the torpedo, blew a gap, and one small group began to move forward.

Lieutenant Colonel Thornton D. Mullins (111th Field Artillery Battalion) crawled along the sea wall, encouraging men to clean the sand off their rifles and start shooting. Each of the self-appointed leaders acted alone, without any idea that others up and down the beach were doing the same.

Courage was not restricted to any one section of the front. Between 8:00 A.M. and 12:00 noon, these small, improvised advances became the pattern, inspiring further bravery. At several points, infantrymen got as far as the top of the bluffs. One 1st Division company worked its way several hundred yards inland.

These first breaks through the beach defenses were so small, however, that the enemy's 352nd Division reported to the German Seventh Army that the Omaha Beach assault had been stopped at the water's edge. Bradley, on board the *Augusta* not far off Omaha, waited anxiously for news. Except for word that Rangers had quickly taken Pointe du Hoe, west of Omaha, Bradley's reports from V Corps were all bad. Noon came, and Bradley was wondering whether the follow-up force—almost as large again as the 34,000-man advance force—should be sent to Utah, or to the British and Canadian zones. Finally, at 1:30 P.M., Bradley received a short, encouraging message from

Gerow: "Troops formerly pinned down on beaches Easy Red, Easy Green, Fox Red advancing up heights behind beaches."

The crisis was passed. By the end of the day, the Allies had two firm beachheads and one weak one on the Normandy coast. By June 8th (D-plus-3) the Allied toe hold was firm, even though the Omaha and Utah forces had not yet linked up.

The Germans continued to worry about a Pas de Calais attack. German troops on the battlefield fought hard, but reinforcements were late—partly because Allied low-level strafing made any movement along the Normandy roads almost suicidal by day. But the Germans were not to be counted out. Rommel was back at his headquarters, and fifteen German divisions were moving up to dispute the issue.

Bradley and Montgomery, however, made good use of the time the Germans allowed them. On June 12th, the 101st Airborne took Carentan, at the base of the Cherbourg peninsula. The beachheads were finally one continuous front. Montgomery pressed hard toward Caen, a city that was supposed to have been taken on D-Day. Rommel committed three armored divisions to hold back the British–Canadian advance. This meant that he couldn't use their tanks for a driving thrust, the standard German counterattack.

Day by day the Allied position slowly improved—despite a storm which began on June 19th, halted

139

unloading operations for four days, and smashed two artificial harbors that had been floated across the Channel to the beaches. The 4th, 79th, and 9th U.S. Divisions moved slowly toward Cherbourg, where the German garrison was resisting, even though it was hopelessly cut off. Cherbourg was pounded from the air. Then the American infantrymen renewed the attack. Finally, on June 27th, the city surrendered.

Rommel and von Rundstedt already knew that the invasion force could not be contained. In fact, they realized it even before the capture of Cherbourg gave Eisenhower the port he needed. Allied progress on the ground was slow, but the buildup of troops and supplies was incredibly fast. Hitler, as usual, forbade his troops to withdraw. He could think of nothing except a mighty counterattack to drive the Allies back into the sea, but he had not given von Rundstedt the forces to make it. Instead, the Fuehrer issued foolish directives that couldn't be carried out. On July 3rd, he flew into a rage because of von Rundstedt's gloomy outlook and replaced him as commander in chief with Field Marshal Gunther von Kluge.

It was only twenty miles from Omaha Beach to St. Lô, on the Vire River. It seemed much farther to the American infantrymen who took the ground—one small Normandy orchard, pasture, or field at a time. The land was a checkerboard divided by hedgerows, walls of overgrown dirt and stone built up over hundreds of years by farmers clearing their fields. These hedgerows served as parapets for the German defenders. Taking each walled field was a little battle.

Soon an American sergeant came up with a brilliant invention—steel prongs welded to the front of a Sherman tank, like a giant pitchfork. The prongs dug in, held down the nose of the tank, and enabled it to butt an opening through the middle of a hedgerow. Even so, by the time five U.S. divisions, led by General Charles H. Gerhardt's 29th, captured St. Lô on July 18th, they hoped they would never see Normandy again.

As July came to an end (D-plus-50), the Allied front was scarcely any farther inland than the pre-invasion plan for D-plus-5. (In Italy, during the same time, the Allied forces had driven Kesselring 150 miles north of Rome.) American, British, and Canadian casualties in Normandy had reached 122,000, a few thousand more than the German losses. Nonetheless Eisenhower had thirty-four divisions in France, most of them in excellent shape. He was ready to break out.

On July 20th, Hitler was at his headquarters in East Prussia. All his generals in the West—von Rundstedt, Rommel, and von Kluge, too—had failed to get him to understand the meaning of the Allied invasion.

A number of Germans, including a group of Hitler's army officers, had long been plotting to assassinate the dictator. They hoped to make peace before Germany was completely shattered by defeat. One of the leaders of the conspiracy was Colonel Klaus von Stauffenberg. He had served as a staff officer in Poland, France, Russia, and North Africa. In Tunisia he had been badly wounded; he had lost his left eye, his right hand, and two fingers of his left hand. He had then been made chief of staff of the Home Army.

Nearly all Hitler's top-ranking officers knew something about the plot. Many of them had been asked to help. Rommel was among them, and so was von Rundstedt. But Rommel had not finally decided to join the conspiracy until July 15th—and then only because Hitler refused to try to open peace negotiations with Great Britain and the United States.

Hitler was holding his noontime staff meeting, which was to hear, among other things, a report by Stauffenberg on new Home Army divisions. Twenty-four officers sat around a large oak table, with Hitler near the middle of one side. Stauffenberg entered the room with a time bomb in his brief case, put it on the floor under the table near Hitler, and then left, pretending he had to make a telephone call.

At 12:42 P.M. a great explosion shattered the room. The roof and part of the walls were blown out and crashed down on the men inside. As the dust and smoke settled a little, Hitler staggered out, leaning on

Field Marshal Wilhelm Keitel's arm. Several of the others were dead or very badly wounded. Hitler's back had been hurt by a falling beam, and his right arm was stiff; his leg was burned and his hair was scorched. But he was not seriously wounded.

The plot had failed. The stout table top and support had shielded the Fuehrer from the bomb. Hitler had an appointment with Mussolini late that afternoon. He was able to keep it. In fact, by then Hitler was in a curiously exalted state—convinced, more than ever, that destiny was protecting him.

Stauffenberg was shot for his part in the plot. The Gestapo rounded up the other chief plotters, and they were either executed or allowed to commit suicide. Hitler's frantic revenge on the plotters continued to the very end of the war. Something like 5,000 Germans —many more than even knew of the plot—were executed. Still more were sent to concentration camps. Rommel was among those given the choice of suicide. He took poison in order to spare his family. Hitler lacked the courage to tell Germany how one of her best generals had died. The cause of Rommel's death was announced as a cerebral embolism, the result of previous "war wounds." He was given a state funeral—which, in fact, he deserved.

12
THE BATTLE FOR FRANCE

The second phase of the Allied invasion called for a change in direction from south to east—a push toward Paris and the calm banks of the Seine River. Von Kluge thought Eisenhower would surely start through Caen. That was the short way and led to flat, open land, good for tanks. Von Kluge had been so busy trying to gather together a mobile reserve force opposite Montgomery at Caen that he had practically ignored the threat from Bradley at St. Lô.

Caen, in fact, was to be the pivot point for a vast, turning attack starting just west of St. Lô.

General Collins' VII Corps (four infantry and two armored divisions) began the offensive on July 25th. All that morning the air throbbed with the sound of

Allied bombers—2,200 of them, including fighter bombers—laying down a carpet of destruction that was supposed to get the ground attack off to an easy start. In spite of the most careful planning, many of the bombs fell short and hit the 9th and 30th divisions. They suffered almost 600 casualties and the whole offensive was thrown off balance. But despite this tragedy, the air attack had successfully blasted a great hole through the hedgerows. One German division had been nearly wiped out.

Collins moved ahead and, on his right, Middleton's VIII Corps moved with him. The 1st Division took Coutances on July 27th. Suddenly von Kluge realized that the west end of his line was crumbling, and he sent two panzer divisions to try to keep Collins from getting to Tessy-sur-Vire. By the last day of the month, Middleton's 6th and 4th armored divisions had raced forty miles, taken Avranches, and were ready to turn west into Brittany.

Since the end of the Sicilian campaign Patton had been in eclipse, mainly because of the slapping incident. He had spent most of the winter at Palermo, an army commander without an army. Eisenhower, however, had not forgotten him. In March, the Supreme Commander had brought Patton to England, and had assigned him a "Third Army" headquarters, but no troops. This was part of the counter-intelligence plan

145

to deceive the Germans into thinking the landings would be in the Pas de Calais area.

Now Patton's painful inactivity was ended. Eisenhower and Bradley knew that a golden opportunity was at hand, and they had always agreed that in an open, moving battle Patton had no equal. The Third Army went into action on August 1st, and Patton was assigned four corps—the VIII, XII, XV, and XX.

Patton turned Middleton's VIII Corps into Brittany, toward the port of Brest. Then he sent his other three corps off in other directions. As far south as the Loire River, columns of XX Corps tanks barreled down the roads without regard for their flanks, their rear, or anything but the job of splitting open enemy positions. XV Corps swung east toward Le Mans, and had almost reached it by August 8th. Then to Patton's dismay, Bradley called a halt to the wide-swinging, spectacular end run.

Bradley had a reason. On orders from Hitler, von Kluge had finally mounted a major counterattack, starting just after midnight on August 7th. The Germans had turned loose seven divisions led by three tank outfits. Their first objective was Mortain, a village at the foot of a rocky hill just south of the town of Vire.

Major General Leland S. Hobbs's 30th Infantry Division had just moved into Mortain, taking over from the 1st Division. One rifle company of the 2nd Battalion of the 120th Infantry Regiment was manning Mortain's three roadblocks—two on the roads into the village from the north, and one on the south. The rest of the battalion's companies were on the rocky hill. As the men were settling down for their first night in the new sector, they heard the roar of tank engines approaching. It was not the noise of Shermans.

Von Kluge was not using any artillery preparation. His lead tanks loomed up out of the darkness and bowled their way through two of the roadblocks. The 2nd SS Panzer Division's twin columns lumbered into Mortain from both the north and the south, pausing only to fire a shell or two through the walls of the old buildings and to spray the path ahead with machine-gun fire. Second Battalion headquarters was overrun. The staff officers scattered into the darkness, diving for whatever cover they could find. Mortain belonged to von Kluge, and the 2nd Battalion was completely isolated from the rest of the division.

The Germans' objective was Avranches, on the sea, only twenty miles west of Mortain. If the daring, surprise thrust could drive that far, Patton's Third Army, as well as those First Army divisions that were already south of the Mortain-Avranches line, would be cut off. Then the Germans could turn north to raise havoc in the Americans' unprotected rear—the supply depots, airstrips, and other installations that had been supporting Bradley's electrifying advance.

The 30th Division reeled from the sudden blow,

but Hobbs's men were anything but routed. The 2nd Battalion companies kept their positions on the hill. They kept fighting. Although Germans had gone far past them, surrender was something the 2nd Battalion did not consider. When relief finally came five days later, the 2nd Battalion's battered lines were surrounded by scores of German dead. And in front of the third roadblock, which had held firm for three fantastic days, more than forty wrecked German vehicles, including several tanks, gave evidence of the Americans' bravery and marksmanship.

Bradley quickly reinforced the crucial Mortain sector with most of four other divisions. He called for help from the air, and rocket-firing R.A.F. Typhoons responded brilliantly. Von Kluge's drive lost momentum a few miles west of Mortain, and it looked as if the stalwart 30th Division, with its reinforcements, would be able to hold the line.

While the outcome was still in doubt, Bradley began to think of counterattacking the counterattack. He was fully aware of the dangers involved in the gamble. To play safe, he could call back some of the First Army divisions that had advanced beyond the Mortain danger point and use them to make sure von Kluge could not reach Avranches. But, on the other hand, the German offensive had put two field armies—100,000 soldiers, including the German infantry from the Pas de Calais area—west of Caen and

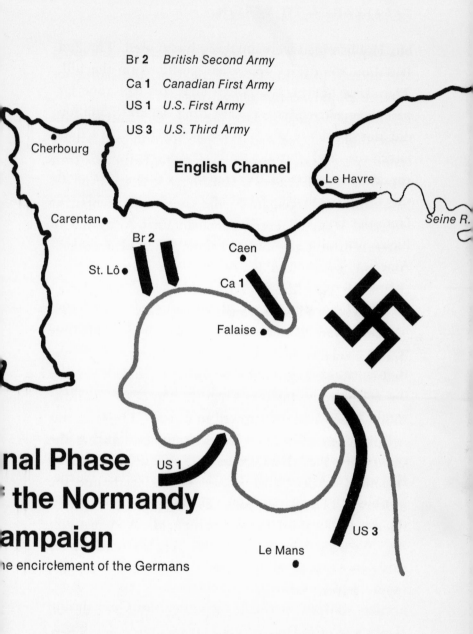

Br **2** *British Second Army*
Ca **1** *Canadian First Army*
US **1** *U.S. First Army*
US **3** *U.S. Third Army*

English Channel

Cherbourg

Le Havre

Carentan

Seine R.

Br **2**

Caen

St. Lô

Ca **1**

Falaise

nal Phase
the Normandy
ampaign

US **1**

US **3**

he encirclement of the Germans

Le Mans

Le Mans. There was a chance that the Germans could be encircled. If so, Bradley thought, the battle for France would be just about over.

Bradley decided to take the risk, to rush east with everything he had—and hope Mortain was strong enough to hold. The order went to Patton to turn Major General Wade H. Haislip's XV Corps from Le Mans toward Argentan. At the same time, Lieutenant General Henry Crerar's Canadian First Army was to advance from Caen toward Falaise. If the plan worked, the two forces would meet like the jaws of a trap, enfolding von Kluge's Fifth and Seventh armies.

All went well with Haislip's Corps. By August 13th it had advanced as far as it was supposed to go. But the Canadians had rough going. Their attack was halted about eight miles north of Falaise. That left an escape route for von Kluge—a gap of twenty-three miles. Soon it was narrowed to fifteen. The Germans managed to get 40,000 soldiers out, but during the next week the Allied ground forces squeezed the trap together, while Allied planes poured death into the pocket. The Allies took 50,000 prisoners; 10,000 Germans lay dead on the battlefield. And many of the Germans who had escaped were rounded up by Patton's Third Army before they could cross the Seine River.

The Germans had suffered an overwhelming defeat. Only bits of the two German armies were left. There was nothing they could do but withdraw from France into Germany.

At the moment of von Kluge's fateful defeat, Hitler had more bad news: the Allied invasion of Southern France had begun on August 15th. It had originally been planned for the same time as the cross-Channel attack, but the Allies did not have enough landing craft for two simultaneous invasions. Lieutenant General Alexander M. Patch's Seventh Army—three American divisions, an airborne task force, and a French commando brigade—hit the coast southwest of Cannes. The Germans had already withdrawn some forces from the area, and their resistance was uneven. Patch pushed vigorously up the Rhone River Valley, heading for Chaumont in central France, where he hoped to join up with Patton's Third Army.

Paris was liberated on August 25th, after a seven-day street battle in which the French civilians tried to free themselves from the German occupying forces. The French 2nd Armored Division, commanded by General Jacques LeClerc, came to the freedom fighters' aid, and sent a column into the center of the city. The people of Paris went wild with joy. They treated the French soldiers' arrival as a great party, even though all morning there was confused fighting at a few places in the city. General von Choltitz, the German commander, decided to disobey

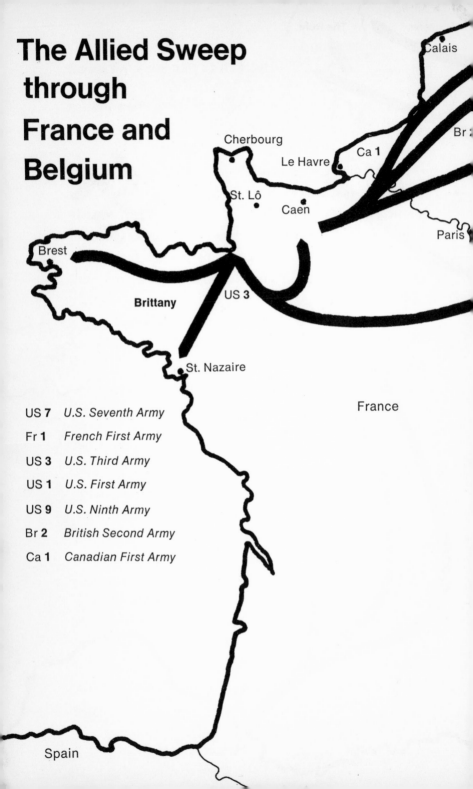

The Allied Sweep through France and Belgium

Calais

Br 2

Cherbourg

Le Havre

Ca 1

St. Lô

Caen

Paris

Brest

Brittany

US 3

St. Nazaire

France

US 7	*U.S. Seventh Army*
Fr 1	*French First Army*
US 3	*U.S. Third Army*
US 1	*U.S. First Army*
US 9	*U.S. Ninth Army*
Br 2	*British Second Army*
Ca 1	*Canadian First Army*

Spain

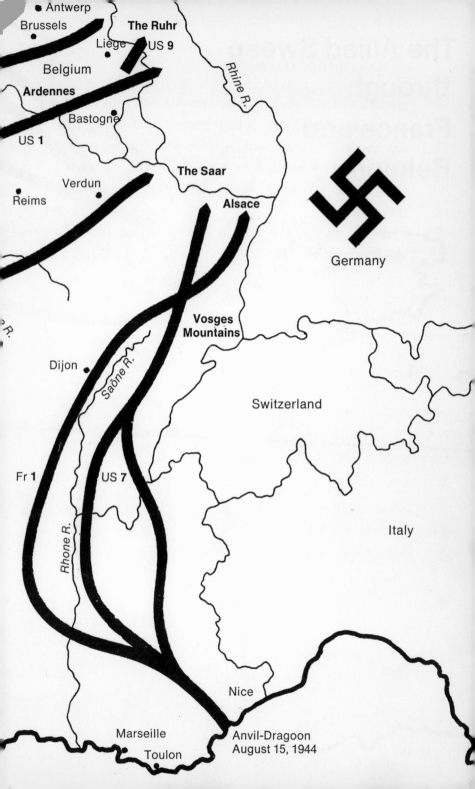

The Allied Sweep through France into Belgium

Antwerp

Brussels

The Ruhr

Liège

US 9

Belgium

Ardennes

Bastogne

US 1

The Saar

Verdun

Alsace

Reims

Germany

R.

Vosges Mountains

Dijon

Saône R.

Switzerland

Fr 1

US 7

Italy

Rhone R.

Nice

Marseille

Anvil-Dragoon
August 15, 1944

Toulon

Hitler's order: "Paris will be transformed into a heap of rubble. The commanding general will defend the city to the last man, and, if necessary, will be buried beneath it." Von Choltitz saw no point in destroying a city the Germans would lose anyhow. He surrendered.

By 12:30 P.M. the French flag was flying from the top of the Eiffel Tower.

13
THE BATTLE OF THE BULGE

Even before Paris had stopped rejoicing, four great Allied armies—Crerar's First Canadian, Dempsey's Second British, Hodges' First American, and Patton's Third American—moved into action north of the Seine. They were racing as fast as they could for the Channel ports, for Antwerp at the head of the Scheldt Estuary, and for the borders of Germany.

Now the advance was going much faster than anyone had expected, and supply calculations had to be drastically revised.

Paris was free fifty-five days earlier than the OVERLORD planners had foreseen. By September 15th, months ahead of schedule, Hodges' First Army was fighting at Aachen inside Germany. It was getting

155

just about half the supplies it needed. Among other things, the ground forces were literally out of gas.

The Germans were about to yield the port of Brest, on the Brittany peninsula. Brest had once been considered an objective second in importance only to the port of Cherbourg. Now it was so far away from the crucial fighting that its devastated port facilities scarcely seemed worth repairing.

On September 4th, the Second British Army entered Antwerp in Belgium, the finest port in all Europe. If only the German Fifteenth Army could be cleared out of the estuary, where the Scheldt River splits into several channels, the port could be used. Then the supply problem would be partly solved.

But Montgomery interested everyone in another scheme: an airborne attack on Arnhem, Holland, sixty-four miles behind the German lines. A British Second Army advance would link up with the airdrop. In one stroke, Montgomery argued, the Allies might cross the Maas, the Waal, and the Lower Rhine rivers, outflank the Germans' defensive West Wall, and perhaps start the Allied forces toward the Ruhr, Germany's great industrial area.

After so many victories, Eisenhower's headquarters underestimated the Germans' remaining strength. Allied strategists thought that von Rundstedt had no more than 15 divisions for the defense of the entire western front. British intelligence estimated that there were at most 100 German tanks in all Holland. The Allies believed the Germans were as good as finished.

Eisenhower approved Montgomery's plan. The three-division (one British, two American) airdrop took place on September 17th. To the airborne troops' dismay, however, two fully equipped German panzer divisions were waiting near the drop zones. The Second Army was unable to get through to rescue the paratroops, and bad weather made it extremely difficult to reinforce or supply them by air. The bold attack was stopped in its tracks, and the 1st British Airborne Division was practically destroyed. No more than 2,500 of its men returned safely. The 101st and the 82nd Airborne also suffered heavy casualties. About all the Allies gained was the knowledge that the Germans were still a fighting force.

Montgomery returned to the pressing business immediately at hand: clearing the Germans out of the Scheldt Estuary. It was far from an easy task. But on November 28th the first Allied supply ship dropped anchor in the harbor of Antwerp.

The supply situation slowly improved—thanks, in part, to an amazing system of truck columns called "The Red Ball Express," which roared from Cherbourg to the front. But the good weather was running out. Both Montgomery and Patton, on the north and south ends of the line, begged Eisenhower for permission to risk everything on "one deep dagger thrust," as Montgomery phrased it, into the heart of Germany. Eisenhower was not impressed. Neither general could suggest exactly what the Allies would do if the spearhead failed to finish off the Germans. SHAEF Headquarters stuck with the idea Eisenhower had had all along: to advance, as the supply situation allowed, on a broad front. The hardest push would start just north of the wooded Ardennes region of Belgium, and continue until the Ruhr district on the far side of the Rhine River fell to the Allies.

By mid-December, all of Eisenhower's seven armies (a new one, Lieutenant General William Simpson's Ninth, had gone into the line between Hodges and Montgomery) were close to the Rhine River. At Strasbourg, Patch's Seventh Army was right on it. The supply situation was greatly improved. Eisenhower was looking forward to renewing the offensive, putting his main effort through Aachen and Julich, on the Roer River.

But the Germans had plans for an offensive of their own.

Von Rundstedt had been restored to command, and had achieved a near miracle since the end of August. Despite the loss of twenty-eight divisions, he had made a line of defense. The line was stretched thin, but it was strong enough to withstand the constant blows falling on it from Nijmegen, Holland, to the Swiss border.

Hitler's latest theory was that the American civilians at home could not accept a horrible defeat. He dreamed of wiping out thirty Allied divisions. Then, he imagined, President Roosevelt would have to yield to vast popular demand, and bring all American forces back from Europe.

On the Eastern Front, the Russians had occupied Rumania and then Bulgaria, and were driving forward, almost unopposed, toward Hungary. In Italy, the Germans had fallen back to their last defensive position across the top of the peninsula. Finland had surrendered to the Russians, endangering all the German troops in Norway and Denmark.

In this crisis, Hitler, to his generals' astonishment, ordered a great attack through the forests of the Ardennes. He wanted to repeat, on a smaller scale, the German offensive which had been a lightning success in 1940.

To gather together a new force for his incredible scheme, Hitler had lowered the German draft age to sixteen and raised it to fifty, and had combed out every possible man from home-front jobs. He now had twenty-five new *Volksgrenadier* (Home Army) divisions for a reserve, and at least six new panzer divisions to add to the striking force.

While Hitler was assembling his attack force in the forests across the Rhine, bad weather hampered Allied air reconnaissance. Expecting no trouble, Eisenhower had thinned out the U.S. VII Corps lines in the Ardennes sector to add strength to his planned offensive north of the Ardennes.

Before dawn on December 16th, the Germans attacked—from Monschau on the north to Echternach on the south. The main effort was made by the Fifth and Sixth Panzer armies in the center. On their flanks, the Fifteenth and Seventh armies went along to protect them from Allied retaliations. Von Runstedt's total attack force added up to 36 divisions.

Middleton's VII Corps was stunned. The Germans advanced rapidly in the center. Yet from the outset the attack did not go as well as the Germans had hoped. Even when they were cut off and surrounded, American units fought superbly. The Germans could not budge V Corps, on the north shoulder of the German advance, and consequently von Rundstedt could not use several roads he had counted on. The 7th Armored Division occupied an important crossroad town, St. Vith, and clung to the position for six days —holding off the whole Sixth German Army.

On December 17th, Eisenhower committed the only two reserve divisions he had: the 101st Airborne to reinforce an armored detachment at Bastogne, and the 82nd Airborne to strengthen the north side of the breakthrough. By December 21st, the 101st, with parts of the 9th and 10th Armored divisions, was cut off and

US **1**   *U.S. First Army*

US **3**   *U.S. Third Army*

Liége

US **1**

Malmédy

Meuse R.

Belgium

St. Vith

Houffalize

Ardennes

Bastogne

Germany

Sedan

US **3**

US **3**

France

Luxembourg

The Battle of the Bulge

December 16, 1944, to January 16, 1945

Route of the German attack

Direction of U.S. counterattack

Area of German penetration

surrounded. The next day Patton began a drive from the south to relieve Bastogne.

The gallant stands of several small units, together with the resistance at Bastogne, gave Bradley the time to shift troops—a total of twenty-nine U.S. and four British divisions—to the Ardennes.

On Christmas Day, the American 2nd Armored Division attacked the 2nd Panzer Division at Celles, not far from the Meuse River, and crushed its advanced units. That was the farthest Hitler's drive got. Late that same afternoon, Patton's 4th Armored Division punched its way through to Bastogne. If General Anthony McAuliffe, the commander of the beleaguered 101st at Bastogne, really answered "Nuts!"— as the American legend tells it—when the Germans demanded his surrender, his confidence proved justified.

The Battle of the Bulge, as the newspaper headlines called it, had cost the Allies 75,000 casualties and delayed the Allied offensive for a month or more.

But sometimes, in a prize fight, a boxer wears himself out in the act of throwing punches. Hitler had hurt the Allies badly, but he had also ruined the German army in the west. Von Rundstedt's casualties were more than 100,000 men—close to every third man in the four armies. The Germans had lost about 1,000 planes, and perhaps 800 tanks.

Some of the forces Hitler lost in the Ardennes had

come from the Eastern Front. There, on January 12th, the Russians launched another offensive. They swept across Poland, captured almost all of East Prussia, and drove deep into Silesia. By January 15th, Marshal Zhukov's First White Russian Army was only fifty miles from Berlin.

14
FINAL VICTORY

The Rhine River was the last natural barrier between Eisenhower's armies and the Ruhr. On paper, the Germans still had sixty divisions prepared to defend it, but Hitler's strength was really far less. Earlier in the war, he would have counted his defenders as perhaps twenty-five divisions. The smaller units of 1945 were filled with untrained recruits and were short of weapons, fuel, and ammunition.

Still, as Eisenhower's final offensive got under way, the Germans resisted fairly strongly between the Roer River and the Rhine. But they had to retreat. They prepared to blow up all the bridges across the Rhine.

On March 7th, Hodges' III Corps reached the Rhine at Remagen, about where von Rundstedt had assembled his attack force for the Battle of the Bulge. The 9th Armored Division advance patrols, leading the way, were astonished to discover that the Ludendorff Bridge had not been blown. The Germans had put detonators and charges in place but the explosives had not gone off.

Lieutenant Karl Timmermann hurried his platoon downhill to the bridge and out onto the span. When they were three-quarters of the way across the bridge, one secondary demolition charge exploded, but little damage was done. As the Germans watched from the far side, the Americans worked to save the structure. Engineers hurried to pull out wires, detach detonators, and remove boxes of high explosive from the bridge's piers. The Allies had a ready-made Rhine crossing!

The immediate question was: how many troops could safely be sent to the far side of the river?

When Bradley heard about this remarkable stroke of luck, he wanted to push across all the forces he had near by—a total of four divisions. He was willing to risk the danger of a German counterattack for the sake of the great prize.

When he checked with Eisenhower, the Supreme Commander suggested that Bradley try to raise the total to five divisions. By March 9th, First Army had a substantial bridgehead, more than three miles deep, across the Rhine, and was building up the strength of the bridgehead force rapidly.

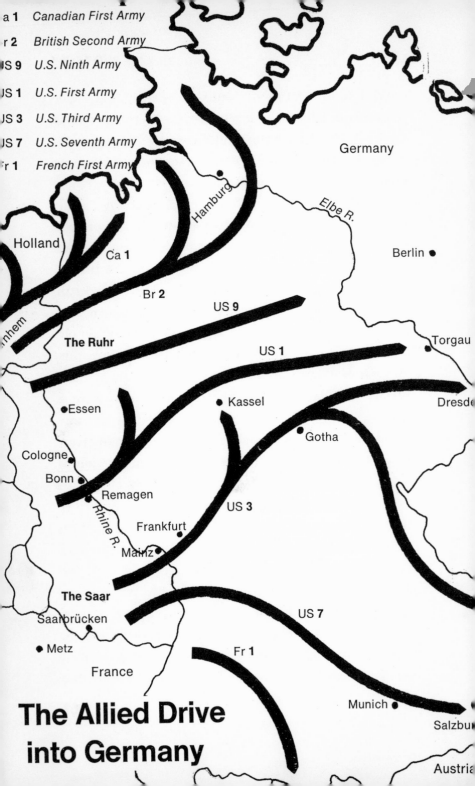

The Allied Drive into Germany

a 1	*Canadian First Army*
r 2	*British Second Army*
US 9	*U.S. Ninth Army*
US 1	*U.S. First Army*
US 3	*U.S. Third Army*
US 7	*U.S. Seventh Army*
r 1	*French First Army*

Germany

Holland

Hamburg

Elbe R.

Berlin

Ca 1

Br 2

US 9

The Ruhr

US 1

Torgau

nhem

Essen

Kassel

Dresde

Gotha

Cologne

Bonn

Remagen

Rhine R.

US 3

Frankfurt

Mainz

The Saar

Saarbrücken

Metz

Fr 1

US 7

France

Munich

Salzbu

Austria

Well to the south of Remagen, Patton was eager to cross the Rhine quickly before the Germans on the far bank had time to organize a strong defense.

"Every day we save," Patton pointed out, "means saving hundreds of American lives."

The Germans thought the logical place for Patton to try a crossing was at Mainz, and they had moved two excellent regiments there to reinforce the defense of the east bank.

Late on March 22nd, the Americans at Mainz began heavy artillery fire, laying down a smoke screen that concealed what they were doing from German observers. The Germans thought their intelligence predictions had been right. But Patton had them completely fooled. The shellfire and the smoke were a trick calculated to draw the defenders' attention away from the real crossing site, Oppenheim, a small river-barge harbor miles to the south of Mainz. As soon as it was completely dark, the leading platoons of the 5th Infantry Division moved quietly down to the river bank. They got into their tiny assault boats in the protected harbor. There was no unusual artillery fire and no preliminary air bombardment. At 10:30 P.M. the 5th Division boats, with a few rafts for heavy weapons and ammunition, began the stealthy crossing.

The Rhine at Oppenheim is not very wide but, to the infantrymen leading the way, the trip seemed eternal. They feared that it was too much to hope that

167

they could reach the far shore without being spotted by a German sentry. And in midstream the slow-moving boats would be an easy target.

But not a single German shot was fired. The 5th Division men were on the east bank, scrambling forward through darkness, before the first German alarm was given. Some of the enemy soldiers, sleeping in farmhouses near the landing place, were taken prisoner before they were fully awake. The attack was such a success that the 5th Division never needed to halt for a reorganization on the far shore. Its leading companies pushed ahead while the assault boats ferried more and more men across. The engineers began to build a two-track bridge, floating on pontoons, across the river.

By noon of the 23rd, the entire 5th Division had made the crossing, and the 90th Infantry Division was following close behind. Long-range German artillery opened fire on the bridge construction, and more than 100 Luftwaffe planes attacked the site. But the defenders were too late. By late afternoon, the bridge was finished and tanks of the 4th Armored Division were moving across it on their way to lead the attack farther east. By dark, the bridgehead was six miles deep and a little more than six miles wide. The Americans had a second major toe hold on the far side of the Rhine, and Patton's total losses had been only eight men killed and twenty-six wounded.

The biggest of the Rhine crossings took place the next day, March 24th. It was at Wesel, just north of the Ruhr district, and it had been planned and mounted with elaborate care. Montgomery's Twenty-First Army Group, with Simpson's Ninth U.S. Army attached, made the great attack, using LCVPs and LCMs hauled halfway across Europe on special trailers. Two thousand Allied cannon fired a tremendous preparatory bombardment.

Eisenhower knew that the Germans had seen many of the preparations for the Wesel attack and assumed the enemy would resist as strongly as possible. As it turned out, the opposition was feeble. On the Ninth Army front, the 30th and 79th divisions led the way across with no more than a few dozen casualties.

That morning, Prime Minister Churchill appeared on the battlefield, looking delighted with the way the operation was going—and scaring the wits out of the staff men responsible for his personal safety.

"My dear general," Churchill said to Eisenhower, "the German is whipped. We've got him. He is all through."

This time the Allied estimate of the situation was correct.

By March 25th, Patton's 4th Armored Division had raced ahead from the Oppenheim bridgehead and was across the Main River at Aschauffenburg. The possibility of a vast double-envelopment of the Ruhr had long been Eisenhower's hope, and his First and Third armies' aggressive successes made its chances look good. Hodges pushed forward out of the Remagen bridgehead, and Patton continued to drive east and then north. From March 29th on, these two great armies were in contact, wheeling north together toward Kassel. At the same time, Simpson's Ninth Army moved east from the Wesel bridgehead, forming the upper jaw of a giant nutcracker that was closing on the Ruhr district. On April 1st, the two American forces met at Lippstadt, near Paderborn. The Ruhr was encircled. Its German defenders, commanded by Field Marshal Walter von Model, were trapped.

Model tried to escape by attacking to the north. He failed. He tried to escape by attacking to the south. He failed there, too.

American artillery ringed the area. It fired day and night, battering the German army and the vast congregation of plants and factories within the area. The Ninth, First, and Third armies squeezed the giant nutcracker tighter and tighter. On April 14th, the eastern half of the Ruhr district gave up. On the 16th, the remainder of the garrison surrendered. The total number of prisoners came to 325,000—even more than all the Germans and Italians captured at the end of the Tunisian campaign.

Hitler had expected Field Marshal Model and his

twenty-one divisions to defend the Ruhr to the last man, but the Germans had held out for only eighteen days.

It was only 150 miles from Kassel to the Elbe River. On April 12th, the day President Roosevelt died— U.S. Ninth Army advance units had begun streaking across the plains to the Elbe. By agreement of the Allies at the Yalta meeting in February, this river was to mark the eastern limit of the American occupation zone of Germany. Eisenhower—to Churchill's dismay —had decided that the Elbe would be the British-American stopping point.

The Russian army was now only thirty miles from Berlin. The British, Canadian, and American forces were racing through Germany, taking ground as fast as they could march. On May 5th, Patton's Third Army was inside the Czechoslovakian border, within striking distance of Prague, the capital. Eisenhower stopped the Third Army, just as he had stopped the Ninth Army on the Elbe.

He was well aware of the political significance of Berlin, Prague, and Vienna. But Eisenhower was a soldier and, as he had told the Combined Chiefs of Staff on April 7th, he did not feel that Berlin should be a major British or American military objective. It had little or no military significance. Eisenhower thought the important remaining job was the destruction of the remnants of the German army. To accomplish it, Eisenhower first wanted to make a thrust to the Elbe near Leipzig; then he wanted to anchor the Allied left flank securely near Lubeck, on the Baltic.

In view of what happened later between Russia and the Western Allies, Eisenhower has often been criticized for not trying to race the Russians to Berlin for the sake of prestige. But it is well to remember that his decision was made from a military point of view that the Combined Chiefs shared.

By the 30th of April, the Russians were fighting their way through the streets of Berlin. Only the day before, Hitler had received word from Italy that Mussolini and his mistress, Clara Petacci, had been caught and shot by Italian rebels. Their bodies were taken to Milan, and hung up by the heels on public display in the Piazzale Loreto.

Hitler had lunch in his underground bunker. He and his wife, Eva Braun, whom he had married the day before, said good-bye to Goebbels, Bormann, and the few others who were still with them. Then they went into their private suite and closed the door. A few minutes later, one shot rang out. Hitler had shot himself in the mouth. Eva Braun had swallowed poison.

On May 6th Admiral Doenitz, whom Hitler had named as his successor, gave General Alfred Jodl authority to sign a complete and unconditional surrender. Jodl signed the papers at 2:41 A.M. on the morning of May 7th. The fighting stopped at midnight, May 8, 1945.

The scene of the surrender was Rheims, France. As soon as the official ceremony was over the weary Eisenhower went right to bed. There was no celebration at his headquarters. But when the news was released to the world, half of the cities of the globe went wild with happiness.

In his "Victory Order of the Day," Eisenhower thanked his soldiers, and their supporters at home, for the help they had given him:

> The route you have traveled through hundreds of miles is marked by the graves of former comrades. Each of the fallen died as a member of the team to which you belong, bound together by a common love of liberty and a refusal to submit to enslavement. Our common problems of the immediate and distant future can best be solved in the same conceptions of coöperation and devotion to the cause of human freedom as have made this Expeditionary Force such a mighty engine of righteous destruction.
>
> . . . Every man, every woman, of every nation here represented has served according to his or her ability, and the efforts of each have contributed to the outcome. This we shall remember—and in doing so we shall be revering each honored grave, and be sending comfort to the loved ones of comrades who could not live to see this day.

INDEX

174

INDEX